Down with boring old food!

© 2007 Rebo International
This publication: © 2007 Rebo Productions b.v., Lisse

www.rebo-publishers.com
info@rebo-publishers.com

Contributors: Sylviane Beauregard, Dominique Bergès, Emmanuèle Carroué,
Véronique Chapacou, Claire Chapoutot, Mijo D'Araujo, Frédérique Despature,
Stéphanie Durand, Anne Lataillade,Gloria Herpin, Elvira Mendes André,
Jacqueline Mercorelli, Brigitte Munoz, Anne Rolland, Aude Toniello
Full-page photos: Raphaële Vidaling
Design: Claire Guigal
Original title: Une souris dans le potage… Recettes et récits de blogs culinaires
© 2006 Copyright SA, 12, Villa de Loucine, 75014, Paris, France
Translation: First Edition Ltd, Cambridge, UK
Editing: Sarah Dunham, Erin Slattery

ISBN: 978-90-366-2174-8

Down with boring old food!

Inventive little recipes for the 21st century

Text: Anna Pavlowitch and Raphaële Vidaling
Photographs: Raphaële Vidaling

 REBO PUBLISHERS

Contents

Ingredients or unexpected liaisons

Experimental Techniques

It's all in the decoration

Introduction

Let us make one thing clear at the start: we really love our grandmothers! And we love beef hash, veal ragout, and apple tart even more. What we are less fond of is the hundredth cookbook repeating the recipes for beef hash, veal ragout, and apple tart... All of those books which sound like they belong in the bottom of the drawer and which have us reheating yesterday's ragout under the pretext of authenticity. When we leaf through a cookbook the main thing we are looking for is ideas. To be inspired, to adjust, to adapt. In this book the ideas which we have gathered together for you are ideas which have been close to our heart for a long time. For what better way is there to stand up to the monument of Tradition with a capital T than with a provocative "why not"?

We are not claiming that these recipes are better than the perennial ones. They are simply a little different and this difference has something of a revival effect. An awakening of the taste buds to an unusual association of flavors or to new ingredients, a visual awakening to food presentation which raises a smile, an awakening of the creative talents in the amateur cook who, as the name of this series suggests, suddenly starts to be worth his "grain of salt" instead of just following traditional recipes as if they were prescriptions.

And why? For the pleasure of it, simple as that. To see, to taste, and, almost like alchemy, even for the pleasure of transforming ingredients, tastes, and colors. We are not beyond seeing cooking as a kind of handicraft, as "creative leisure" you could say, which as such is a source of satisfaction. Testing a gelatin dessert with seaweed powder, drying flowers on the radiator, smoking fish yourself in a pan, tasting raw vegetables which are usually served cooked, or cooking an exotic fruit which you do not even know the name of; these are the things we enjoy doing. And if it doesn't quite work out, never mind, we will still have learned something in terms of cooking method, the quantity of spices, the order of the preparation, etc. If it is a success, so much the better! And then comes the sharing part. "Taste this, I invented it!" All of the following recipes have been tested, often several times, by us, they have been tasted by us, and have been tasted by others. Some recipes were left out for being just too different, too mundane, too unappetizing… But many have been retained. Are they perfect?

Certainly not: we are neither chefs nor cooking professionals. But if we have chosen to publish them it is because, in their own way, each of them finds its justification in a (good) little innovative idea, be it in terms of texture, association, or presentation. Innovative in relation to other cookbooks, not necessarily in relation to the exquisite inventions of the great chefs. All of the photographs were taken without the use of tricks, coloring, lacquer, without retouching, and using natural light… unlike most other cookbooks! All of the dishes you see in the photographs were cooked in an ordinary kitchen where they were then photographed and, finally, tasted. Simple as that. For you the reader this is, in fact, your guarantee: what you will end up with on your plate can only but resemble what you see on these pages. Unless of course you have taken other liberties with the recipes, something which we can only encourage! And without taking into account the random aspect which is the spice of life anyway. If we are to take up a position against the stuffiness of a specific tradition then we do need to pose the question about modernity in cook-

ing. What does it constitute? How do the recipes of the 21st century define themselves in relation to those which came before? The answer is a multifaceted one. In the first instance one would like to say: open mindedness. If tradition is defined as a passing down through the centuries from one pair of hands to the next, thus forming a long chain, then modernity in cooking consists of breaking this chain in order to link it to others, of opening up the hands so that they autonomously grasp the inspiration on the left and on the right.

This is why one of the chapters of this book is titled "Ingredients or Unexpected Partnerships." These days one often hears talk of fusion food, of world food, to describe the mix of culinary cultures. It is true that exotic ingredients are a real stimulus for inspiration: Chinese artichokes, chayotes from the Antilles, teriyaki sauce, acorn syrup, seaweed, Chinese mushrooms, carambola, pomegranates... Yet, there are also all sorts of "local" ingredients from the traditional register which are fun to rediscover (pumpkin, verbena, Romanesco cabbage, Jerusalem artichoke, parsnips, dried meadowsweet, alfalfa...) or which belong to those

groups of products considered to be less desirable or to be reserved for children (Fraises Tagadas sweets, soda, condensed milk, sherbet, fruit jelly...).

The other response to the question of modernity is again the notion of a "grain of salt" being added to a pre-existing basis. Nothing is created *ex nihilo*, we know that: all art progresses through the modification, extension, or adjustment of that which existed before. The same applies to cooking. That is why we thought it would be fun to call the first chapter "Classics Remixed." As with Oulipien texts these are creations under constraint: to move away from a well-known dish and to

add a small touch which transforms it. The famous ragout takes on the aroma of anise and a surprising presentation, its cousin the hash, renounces its traditional beef and combines with duck and potatoes; ham and endives shrug off its béchamel sauce and reappears in full bloom, etc.

The third chapter is called "Experimental Techniques" because cooking is not simply a matter of ingredients but also of preparation methods which can be inventive to a greater or lesser degree. Playing the sorcerer's apprentice we have therefore tried to flavor eggs through their shells, to liven up a cocktail by crumbling sherbet over crushed ice, to invent a dish served in thermal layers, to make pseudo maki sushi without rice and without nori seaweed, to use herbal teas with-

out water, to transform vegetable peelings into delicately crisp petals, to marinate fish in alcohol, etc. More often than not they are suggestions; we have taken the first step and it is up to you to take the next one, fine-tuning these attempts. Is that not the way scientific discoveries take place? We like to define cooking at our level as manual leisure, as artistic expression, but also as pseudo-scientific tinkering. With a touch of molecular gastronomy à la Hervé This and, of course, gastronomic innovation à la Ferran Adrià, even though we are not claiming to be in the same league…

By way of a conclusion, some visual enjoyment with a chapter titled "It is all in the decor." A modest title which almost sounds defensive given the modernity challenge with which we are faced. It is all in the decor, this means that we are not claiming to present particularly original taste associations: chocolate-strawberry, scallops-orange, pear-blue… On the contrary, we are convinced that it is sometimes enough to change the appearance

of dishes in order to modify the gustatory perception. Hence rose-colored spaghetti, an orchid-shaped mushroom on a pork chop, a garden of alfalfa grown on the plate itself, a brioche transformed by baking parchment decorated with an edible children's drawing, little individual volcanoes erupting with strawberries, etc. For ultimately, the counterpart to tradition is also a certain playfulness of spirit, a kind of "playing with food," how ever you phrase it, and which neverthe-less retains the respect for food. Respect for food, yes; for the rules, no. Looking at it from a new, alternative, and curious angle, without being stuck on the tread-mill of routine. Our recipe motto in summary: peel your rules and regulations and throw them away, make a note of your ideas, mix your influ-ences, marinate them in the juices of everyday life, adjust the seasoning and the powdered chance, leave to rest, and enjoy with friends...

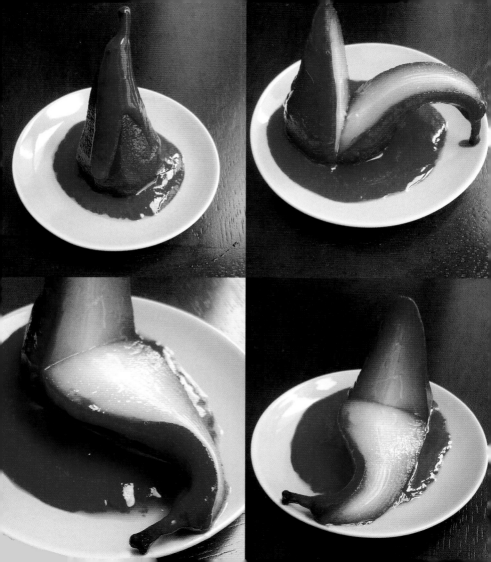

What can you find on the Internet ?

Rare and original products at www.monmarchand.com.

We have been out looking…
· **liquid butter caramel**, for spreading on pancakes, for sweetening an apple compote with Calvados, or even to shorten the preparation time for Caramel Pineapple Cream (p. 84).
· **gomasio**, which is nothing more than sesame salt. Absolutely divine, it is a great replacement for sea salt.
· **nettle mustard**, to transform the taste of a broiled steak into a deliciously stinging moment.
· **grapefruit cookies**, both crunchy and acidic. They can be crumbled over a strawberry salad for an express summer crumble.

Forgotten vegetables and refined tableware at www.epicurieux.com.

We were tempted with…
· the **mini-Chinese artichokes, the Jerusalem artichokes, or the capers in vinegar**, from among the range of forgotten vegetables (because there is nothing more modern than that which is too old to be a classic). Serve with cold meats instead of cornichons (pickles).
· the famous **Rödel sardines**, the Rolls-Royce of canned sardines! To enjoy as they are, with an aperitif, on toast.
· the concentrates called *à la barbe à papa*, **in cornflower blue or poppy red**. A little water, several grams of agar-agar, and you will get the most extraordinary gelatin candies…
· the **bitter almond extract**, almost unobtainable commercially. A few drops of

this elixir transforms fromage blanc or an almond cream (combine chopped almonds with milk and 2 or 3 drops of the extract).

First class pasta at www.ultimapasta.com.

We could not resist…
- real white pasta including the unbelievable **Matites**, large cylinders each measuring 41/2 to 6 inches (12 to15 cm). Serve just 5 to 6 per person.
- the **truffle tagliatelle**, serve with a slice of foie gras or fresh salmon.
- the **Dischi Volanti**, little snails whose shape holds the sauce and does not let it go.

Jelly for any meal at www.fruitine.com.
More than two hundred different jelly flavors which go far beyond the scope of breakfast. Some examples :
- **yellow plums in sweet and sour vanilla and gewürztraminer** (white wine from Alsace) with an aperitif.
- **with herbs**: anise, fennel, rosemary, China tea, to serve with white meats or with baked fish.
- **with Beaujolais**, to serve with broiled steaks.

Condiments and cooked meals from the Middle Ages at www.la-cour-des-saveurs.com.
Here they are not even talking about your grandmother's grandmother! On offer are baskets decorated in the style of the era containing: **Chicken with Dates and Prunes, Venison Casserole, or even Spiced Rabbit Terrine**. Shows you that cooking, like fashion, is a never-ending cycle.

What can you find at an organic food specialist?

Extraordinary pasta

In all shapes, made from all kinds of flour, and in all flavors. And of such deliciously good quality that you simply need to add olive oil or a drop of cream, some salt, and a few turns of the pepper mill… in order to be able to delight the kids and astound the adults.

Nettle tortillas: no, they do not sting! That's why it is fun to serve them with a tomato sauce livened up with a dash of Tabasco. Or, if you want to be even more adventurous, sprinkled with kiwi seeds with their dry, peppery taste. Peel and mash 2 kiwis, pass the flesh through a strainer, and keep the seeds. A little cream and you are done.

Quinoa-carrot pasta shells: such a great orange color it would be a shame to hide them under a thick sauce. A few little bits of butter and the zest of half an orange are enough. The perfect accompaniment to scallops à l'orange (p. 148).

Kamut with lemon, green tea, or ginger: the perfect example of a pasta which transforms any boring old fillet or creamed chicken dish.

Mini half-stars: minuscule stars with five points! They are cooked in 4 minutes and are so pretty you can use them to decorate your plates. You simply have to have enough of them and sprinkle them around as you would chives or chopped parsley.

Multicolored lentils

Beluga lentils: these superb little black grains from Canada are very easy to cook in 20 minutes over low heat once you have rinsed them and brought them to a boil. Season with a little butter, a dash of soy sauce, and a sprinkle of crushed dried seaweed; they are perfect with broiled pork or baked fish.

Green lentils: these green and blue striped lentils do not need to be soaked. Cooking them for 20 to 30 minutes in 3 times their volume of water will suffice. Served with a tomato sauce and pieces of sun-dried tomatoes they make a tasty vegetarian dish.

Pink lentils: when raw they are pink-orange and turn a transparent beige after cooking for 20 minutes in 2 to 3 times their volume of water. They do not "hold" while cooking but rather disintegrate into a sort of grainy puree. Their sweet flavor means you can use them for desserts (p. 86) but they are just as delicious in a cream sauce. You simply need to add, in equal parts, chicken bouillon (as a cube) and cream.

Seeds for sprinkling

Sesame seeds: originating from Africa, sesame seeds can be sprinkled over apple crumble (once cooked), Crème Brulée (before caramelizing), or over a green salad (in a lemon vinaigrette). They can also just as easily be incorporated into a cookie dough.

Poppy seeds: blue poppy seeds are traditionally used by bakeries where they are simply sprinkled over the bread dough before baking. You can also add them to a breadcrumb mixture to transform a Wiener Schnitzel or chicken nuggets.

Flowers for infusing

Mallow: delicate little violet-colored flowers, they color the water they are soaked in blue. For making a syrup or a surprising gelatin dessert (p. 124).

Meadowsweet: to infuse in milk as you would a vanilla bean. It transforms custards and creams by giving them a pretty amber color and a cookie-like flavor (p. 126).

And plenty of other types of dried plants: lavender, eucalyptus, verbena, roses, orange blossom...

Exotic produce

Wild rice: originating from Canada, wild rice needs to be cooked for quite a long time (55 minutes in 2 times its volume of water), but the end result lends a touch of refinement (and color!) to any dish. Its delicate flavor goes particularly well with fish fillets.

Seaweed: you can find a number of varieties pre-packed (in the refrigerated section), in jars – in oil–or even dried. They have been used in Japanese cuisine since time immemorial. Dried and then rehydrated or fresh, they are perfect with pasta or a green salad (in a lemon vinaigrette).

Agar-agar: A magical seaweed which functions as a fast-working gelling agent. You simply need to heat it in liquid at a ratio of 0.07 ounces (2 grams) per 2 cups (500 ml). It gels slowly as it cools. Agar-agar is completely neutral in flavor and can be used in the widest variety of mixtures. You can alternate the color layers (p. 118) or set small pieces of fruit in the agar.

… And in an Asian delicatessen?

Teriyaki sauce: somewhat more subtle than ordinary soy sauce, it is also sweet and sour. You can use it in the Japanese style for marinating meat which you are then going to broil or, as we have done, for soaking eggplant (p. 110). You can also brush chicken kebabs with it before browning them under the broiler.

Wasabi: served with soy sauce and thin slices of marinated ginger to accompany raw fish. It is a kind of very strongly flavored horseradish and is pale green in color; it is used in small quantities as a condiment. Combined with crème fraîche or sour cream, it makes an interesting alternative to mustard. It can also be combined with oil and vinegar (cider vinegar) to make an explosive vinaigrette.

Rice noodles: delicious and ready in just a few minutes, they are available in all shapes, plain or flavored, (crab, shrimp…). Place in a pan of boiling beef or vegetable bouillon at the last minute and they will cook without having to be on the stove (but you must cover with a lid or an upturned plate). Boiled then rinsed under cold water straight away and seasoned with olive oil, lemon, a little white sugar, and chopped ginger, they are wonderful in salads.

Rice flour: makes a breadcrumb mixture very crispy. Just add to the breadcrumbs in equal parts.

Miso soup mix: this is soup in a package. Of course you can use it as such to make a light, flavorsome soup, but there are even more things to do with it! If you mix 2 tablespoons of this powder with mayonnaise and crème fraîche or sour cream in a small bowl you will have a very original sauce as a dip for raw vegetables (carrots, cucumber, baby corn, radishes…).

Five spice powder: this is a mixture of Chinese pepper, cloves, fennel, cinnamon, and star anise. Sprinkled over meat or chopped onions or shallots (1 tablespoon for 1 lb 2 oz (500 g) of meat or vegetables), it has a flavor which is both subtle and strong. We have used it in our duck confit hash (p. 46).

Oyster sauce: this is an example of the kind of Asian product where the name is a little unsettling and can discourage even the best of intentions! Especially if you mention the fact that this sauce is brown and gelatinous and that it should be added to pieces of meat or fish at the end of cooking. However, it would be a real shame to stick with this apprehension because, not only does it not have the taste of crustaceans, it thickens and gives meat pies a very special taste. It works as a flavor enhancer and brings out the flavor of the ingredients which it coats in a delicate caramel colored sauce.

Classics Remixed

Cooking in the infinitive

To dare.
This is the key word.
Nothing is impossible, nothing
is forbidden, cooking is an area of
absolute freedom. It would be too
much of a shame not to make the most
of that. To start with you should make
your dishes in small quantities and test
the results yourself, but you will
soon have those around you
begging to be your guinea
pigs.

To have fun.
There is nothing worse than a
cook who takes him- or herself too
seriously. It is, however, the prerogative of
the perfect domestic goddess who, brought
up from a young age with the "Manual of
Bourgeois Cooking," would not even conceive
of changing a comma in Aunty Annie's
casserole recipe. Do you know that there
are chefs who serve carrot clouds, foie
gras in powder form, or vegetable
candies?

To experiment.
There are no forbidden or
unnatural combinations. The
young chef Katsumi Ishida has no
qualms about combining beef
cheek in wine with fillet of bass,
with amazing results. Let pleasure be your only guide, your
only compass.

To astound.
Any means of reawakening
the senses is good. Change the
usual order of service, serve your
meal the other way round! Suggest a
red wine (something refreshing from
the Loire Valley) with the mussels and a
white wine (dry and fruity) with the
cheeseboard. Come up with new
ways of presenting your food,
new ways of eating, new
rituals…

To mix.
To be able to grow and develop
in the face of culinary tradition
means you need to be curious about
other cuisines. If others had not done
the same a long time ago we would
not even have potatoes, tomatoes,
or chocolate!

To simplify.
No, cooking is not reserved for
"those who know." No, it is not too
late to start. Yes, you can make very
good food by shopping at the grocery
store. And nobody is either gifted or
not gifted in the kitchen, it is simply
a case of being curious and
wanting to do it.

Little ginger cakes à l'orange with duck rillettes

We all know duck à l'orange. Ginger cake with foie gras is being served in restaurants more and more. This recipe is halfway between these combinations: little homemade ginger cakes with a strong orange flavor. The duck rillettes in bite-size portions are somewhat "stronger" than foie gras so it can stand up to the spices. This can be served as a festive season appetizer or as a special dish for a lazy Sunday evening in winter...

For 4 individual cakes

- I orange
- 5 tbsp honey
- I small cinnamon stick
  (or I/2 tsp ground cinnamon)
- I/2 tbsp ground ginger
- I/2 tbsp ground nutmeg
- I tbsp green anise
- 2 cloves
- 2 tbsp (25 g) butter
- 5 tbsp milk
- 3/4 cup (125 g) whole wheat flour
- 2 tbsp baking powder
- I small jar of duck rillettes

Remove the zest from the orange. Place in a pan with I/3 cup + I I/2 tablespoons (100 ml) water, honey, and the spices. Reduce over gentle heat for 10 minutes, or longer if necessary, to obtain a syrup. Preheat the oven to 350 °F (180 °C). Remove the cloves and cinnamon stick from the pan. Add the butter. Once it has melted, remove the pan from the heat. Add the milk and squeeze the orange, then add the juice to the mixture. Add the flour and baking powder and mix well. Pour the dough into nonstick (or greased and floured) mini cake pans. Bake for about 30 minutes: the cakes should have risen and should be browned and cooked through. Serve either warm or cold with a portion of duck rillettes.

Nut and Parmesan ravioli

Did you know that the word ravioli comes from the French word for turnip because, on fasting days, the meat filling was replaced with turnips? Our nut version is therefore a return to the vegetarian origins of this dish. Once filled they look like little savory candies in a cream bath… The diced Parmesan, barely heated, retains its shape and is just slightly melted. One point, however: making this pasta at home takes a lot of time and shaping them into little rounds and cubes does require patience. To be kept for dinners with your loved one and not for a big spread with your friends!

For 2 servings
- 7/8 cup (100 g) flour
- 1 egg
- Salt and freshly ground black pepper
- 2 tbsp olive oil
- 1 oz (25 g) Parmesan (not grated)
- 1/4 cup (30 g) shelled nuts
- 1/3 cup +1 1/2 tbsp (100 ml) cream
- Few sprigs of chives

Combine the flour, the whole egg, a pinch of salt, and the oil. Knead for several minutes: the dough should no be sticky and should become elastic. Wrap in plastic wrap and let rest at room temperature for 1 hour. In the meantime, dice the Parmesan. Divide the dough into several portions and roll out each one using a rolling pin, so that the dough is as thin as possible. Cut the dough into strips and use to wrap a whole nut and a cube of Parmesan. Let the rounds and cubes dry at room temperature for at least 1 hour (or else overnight). Place them in a large quantity of boiling water and cook for 3 minutes. Drain, place in a soup bowl, pour the cream over them, sprinkle with chopped chives, season with salt and pepper, and serve.

Roasted bone marrow with dried figs

Eating bones, what a strange idea! Perhaps in prehistoric times, or even in Rabelais' day, but in the 21st century? It is nevertheless an interesting experience, especially if you cook them like this: think of the bones themselves as a small platter and the fig pate as the lid. The marrow cooks in a vacuum which makes it extremely tender... You remove the lid with a teaspoon and spoon out the contents. It suddenly becomes very civilized! You can serve them as an appetizer or with an aperitif, like hard-cooked eggs, with toast on which each guest can spread the filling, or even together with a piece of broiled steak.

For 4 servings
· 2 tbsp olive oil
· 8 large dried figs
· 8 marrow bones
· Salt and freshly ground black pepper

Preheat the oven to 450 °F (230 °C). Grease an ovenproof dish with 1 tablespoon of oil. Cut the figs in two and remove the flesh using the tip of a knife. Place the bones flat in the dish and cover with the fig flesh. This is like a kind of brown pate which you can spread easily with your fingers. Season with salt and pepper. Reduce the oven temperature to 350 °F (180 °C) and cook for 30 minutes.

Raw turnip rémoulade

As children many of us used to beg for a piece of raw turnip from our mothers or grandmothers while they were preparing a vegetable soup. So, as adults, why do we insist on seeing these juicy, slightly sweet, and subtle tasting tidbits as a spongy, flavorless mass? The cause of this misdeed is: cooking! As an alternative to the banal celeriac rémoulade of the canteen here is raw turnip on a bed of corn salad.

For 4 servings
· 2 lb (1 kg) turnips
· 1 small bowl of mayonnaise
· 1 tbsp strong mustard
· Salt and freshly ground black pepper
· 1 package (9 oz/250 g) corn salad
· 4 tbsp olive oil

Peel and grate the turnips. Wrap them in a dish cloth and wring them out so that you get all of the water out. Combine the mayonnaise with the mustard, and season with salt and pepper. Pour the mixture over the grated turnip and mix together. Wash and dry the corn salad; keep the sprigs whole. Place a dollop of the turnip rémoulade in the center of each of the 4 plates, surround with sprigs of corn salad, and drizzle with 1 tablespoon of oil.

Endive roses with honey

Endives with ham is a classic of French and Belgian cooking. This revised version does away with the béchamel, which covers up all the shapes like a blanket of snow... or wool. The rehabilitated endive is a lot sexier if you keep the arrangement of the leaves. To show off its shape to the best advantage we chose the red endive, a variety which comes from the Chioggia region and which is becoming more and more readily available at markets, but the flower works just as well with a white endive. However, this recipe does require some skill. It is better to take the risks of grating into account and to aim for just 3 roses per endive which allows you to waste a couple.

For 2 servings (6 flowers)
· 2 endives (red if possible)
· Runny honey
· 6 slices of bacon
· 2 tbsp olive oil

Cut a section about 1/2 inch (1 cm) wide from each endive. Remove the base and keep the tip for something else (it wilts when cooked). Place the oil in a skillet. Carefully place each piece of endive in the skillet. Drizzle 1/2 tablespoon of honey over each of them. Cook over gentle heat for 20 minutes. Remove the endive flowers one by one with a fork and place on some paper towels. Place the bacon slices in the skillet you have just used and return to high heat for several minutes, turning the bacon over in the honey. Arrange the slices of caramelized bacon on the plates and place an endive flower on each of them, using the prettiest ones. Serve immediately.

Veal ragout with anise

It is difficult to get more traditional than veal ragout! However, to the disapproval of the purists, it is possible to give it the almost exotic flavor of anise with fennel, reinforced by a nonalcoholic aperitif (easily obtainable, inexpensive, and very practical). What's more, the sensual shape of the fennel allows a certain audacity in the presentation. If both halves are firm then it will hold well and it is up to each guest to undo it so that the ragout spreads over the rice.

For 4 servings

· 4 nice fennel bulbs
· 2 carrots
· 1 onion
· 1 pear
· 1 3/4 lb (800 g) veal without fat
· Olive oil
· 1 bouillon cube
· 1 clove
· 1 small glass of nonalcoholic anise liqueur (or 3 tbsp of green anise, or else 3 star anise)
· 7 tbsp (100 g) crème fraîche or sour cream
· 1 cup (200 g) long-grain rice
· Salt and freshly ground black pepper

Remove the hard part at the base of each fennel bulb, then remove and discard the outer layer. Carefully remove the next two layers of each bulb and keep (in pairs) for the garnish. Dice the rest, and then dice the carrots, onion, pear, and meat. Place the onion and meat in a pan with a little oil. As soon as the meat starts to brown, cover with water and dissolve the bouillon cube in it. Add the vegetables, clove, and anise. Bring to a boil and cook, uncovered, over gentle heat for 45 minutes (or longer). Cook the rice and then drain. Just before serving, adjust the consistency by draining off the bouillon, if necessary, and add the crème fraîche or sour cream. Season with salt and pepper. Cover each plate with rice. Put the fennel bases together in pairs. Place a ladleful of ragout in each and serve the rest in a dish.

Stuffed chayote

To be honest, the filling used in this dish is nothing special, except for the cashew nuts which give it the crunchiness. The idea is simply to replace the tomatoes or the zucchini, which are traditionally used with a less common vegetable, which lends itself to stuffing: the chayote (for me reminiscent of that part of my childhood spent in Martinique). They are also called chou-chou and are becoming increasingly available at markets and in specialty grocery stores. Most recipes have you remove the flesh and boil it. However, it is also good eaten whole, scraping out the flesh and leaving the skin.

For 2 servings
· 2 chayotes
· I garlic clove
· I shallot
· Oil
· 2 slices of ham
· 2 small steaks, ground
· 5 oz (150 g) mushrooms
· Scant 1/2 cup (50 g) cashew nuts
· Salt and freshly ground black
  pepper

Wash the chayotes. Cut them in two lengthwise and place in a pan of boiling water for 10 minutes. In the meantime, dice the garlic and the shallot. Place in a skillet with a little oil. Add the ham, cut into small pieces, and the ground meat, breaking it up with your fingers. Cook over high heat for several minutes, stirring from time to time. Wash and dice the mushrooms. Add them to the skillet. Coarsely chop the cashew nuts and add to the skillet. Season with salt and pepper. Drain the chayotes. Remove the hard core. Place each half in an ovenproof dish. Stuff them with the mixture in the skillet and place the rest of the stuffing around them. Cover with aluminum foil and keep warm in the oven until you are ready to serve.

Veal roulades
with lemon and peanut butter

Roulades, definitely the cuisine of another era but we love them just the same! And what we love most about this dish is that it looks like a little present with a surprise inside. To make sure that the surprise is even more appetizing we suggest replacing the sausage meat with a vegetarian filling, somewhat sweet due to the onions, and with the peanut butter giving it an American touch.

For 4 servings
· 4 small onions
· Olive oil
· 4 tbsp peanut butter (preferably crunchy)
· 4 veal scallops, very thin
· Salt and freshly ground black pepper
· 1 lemon
· 4 slices of ginger cake
· 1 egg
· 4 tbsp nuts, coarsely chopped

And why the ginger cake? Because some traditional recipes include breadcrumbs. Sounds like a great stuffing doesn't it?

Peel and slice the onions. Sauté them in a skillet, covered, with a little oil for 20 minutes. In the meantime, spread the peanut butter over the scallops. Season with salt and pepper. Remove the lemon zest and sprinkle over the scallops. Crumble the ginger cake over the onions. Combine the egg with the nuts. Spread this mixture over the scallops. Roll them up and tie with string. Brown them in a pan with a little oil. Add 1 1/4 cups (150 ml) of water and the lemon juice. Cook over gentle heat for 30 minutes (or longer). Remove the string with some scissors before serving the roulades together with creamy mashed potatoes flavored with lemon, for example.

Braised beef à l'orange

Braised beef is one of those classics which is so classic that one tends to forget that it exists (just like one forgets good old Balzac dozing in front of the library). So, we have decided to revive it! And what better way than with a double dose of vitamin C? The orange juice and zest gives the sleeping beauty the refreshing allure of a mischievous young girl.

For 4 servings

· 2 lb (1 kg) beef knuckle (shoulder will also do, or a combination of both)
· 4 large shallots (or 6 small)
· 3 tbsp olive oil
· Salt and freshly ground black pepper
· 2 organic oranges
· 1 small carton tomato concentrate

Cut the meat into large cubes of more or less equal size (about 2 1/2 inches/6 cm square). Peel the shallots and cut them into quarters lengthwise. Cook the meat and shallots in oil for 5 minutes until they start to brown. Season with salt and pepper. Add the juice of the 2 oranges and the zest of one of them. Use a vegetable peeler if you do not have a zester, taking care not to remove too much of the white pith. Add the tomato concentrate, stir, and then add enough water to just cover the pieces of meat. Cook over gentle heat for 3 hours if using an ordinary pan or only 1 hour in a pressure cooker. Serve with fresh pasta.

NB: this dish tastes even better when reheated and can be frozen for a long time. It is therefore good for preparing in large quantities.

Duck hash with sweet potatoes

This is a dish full of melting softness: the customary hash made from the "leftover meat from the refrigerator" has been replaced by duck confit (which, when cooked, takes on the consistency of marzipan) and the sweet potato is deliciously sweet and not too sticky. And finally, as a special bonus, the recipe can be made in the blink of an eye.

For 4 servings
- 1 lb 2 oz (500 g) sweet potatoes
- 1 jar of duck confit containing at least 2 pieces
- 4 shallots
- 2 tbsp olive oil
- 2 tbsp five-spice powder
- Salt and freshly ground black pepper
- 1/3 cup + 1 1/2 tbsp (100 ml) cream
- 4 tbsp breadcrumbs

Preheat the oven to 450 °F (230 °C). Peel the potatoes, slice, and cook in a pan of boiling water for 20 minutes. Wipe the pieces of duck confit to remove the fat covering them, then remove the meat from the bones (the meat comes away very easily) and cut into small pieces. Sauté the chopped shallots with the oil in a skillet. Add the five-spice powder, season with salt and pepper, and cook over gentle heat for an additional 10 to 15 minutes, then combine with the duck hash. Once the sweet potatoes are cooked, drain them and mash with a fork while adding the cream. Place in ramekins with the duck and shallot mixture on top (just up to 3/4 full) and then another layer of sweet potato. Finish by sprinkling 1 tablespoon of breadcrumbs over each ramekin. Reduce the oven temperature to 350°F (180°C) (broiler position if possible) and reheat for 10 minutes.

Pork chops in milk and cinnamon

Pork chops are traditionally served with mustard or a cream sauce... There is nothing to stop you replacing the mustard with cinnamon. The dish then gains a delicate taste, which again proves that there are no spices destined solely for savory dishes and others for desserts.

For 4 servings
· 2 cups (1/2 liter) milk, lowfat
· 4 tbsp ground cinnamon
· 4 pork chops
· Salt and freshly ground black pepper
· 2/3 cup (150 ml) crème fraîche or sour cream

Heat the milk (do not let it boil) with 3 tablespoons of cinnamon. Let the mixture cool, pour over the meat, and marinate at room temperature for 1 hour. Heat a skillet (without oil) and place the pork chops in it. Pour half of the cinnamon milk over them, reduce the heat to medium, and cook until the liquid has almost disappeared (about 10 minutes). Sprinkle the rest of the cinnamon over the pork chops and cook for a few more minutes on each side. Season with salt and pepper, place the meat on the plates or on the serving dish, and, using a wooden spoon, deglaze the skillet with the crème fraîche or sour cream. Coat the pork chops with the cream and serve with rice or pasta.

NB: do not leave the meat to marinate in the flavored milk for more than 3 hours (we have tested it); it will be more tender but it starts to lose its flavor...

Scallops cassolette with pecans and bacon

Scallops with sugared nuts... why not? To make this dish it is essential to caramelize the pecan nuts otherwise they will absorb the crème fraîche or sour cream and become soft, while the interesting thing about this recipe is precisely this meeting of opposites: crunchy, sugared pecans and tender scallops with cream and bacon.

For 4 servings
· 3 tbsp dark brown sugar
· Scant 1 cup (100 g) pecans
· 3 lb (1.5 kg) scallops
· Generous 3/4 cup (200 ml) cream
· 3 tbsp ground nuts
· Salt and freshly ground black pepper
· 7 oz (200 g) diced bacon
· A few sprigs of chives

Make a caramel by combining the sugar with 3 tablespoons of water over gentle heat. Stir. Once the sugar has melted added the pecans and stir for an additional minute. Remove the nuts from the syrup and place on a plate, taking care to keep them apart from one another so they do not stick together. Wash the scallops thoroughly under cold running water. Discard any that are open and place the others in a pan. Add 2/3 cup (150 ml) of water and heat over high heat for 3 minutes until all the mussels have opened. Reduce the heat. In a bowl, combine the cream and the ground nuts. Season generously with salt and pepper and pour over the scallops. Stir well so that all the scallops are covered in the cream. Sauté the diced bacon in a skillet and add to the scallops with the pecans. Sprinkle with chopped chives just before serving.

NB: you can use other nuts if you cannot find pecans.

Lazy pears with blackberry cream and raspberry coulis

Pears have been given all sorts of names including Poires Belles-Hélène and "Pink Pebble," one which goes back to the Renaissance. There is nothing pebble-like about this recipe, on the contrary. To make these pink pears with pink fruit we have adapted the very classic recipe for pears in wine by adding blackberry cream and suggesting a raspberry coulis as an accompaniment. When cut in two the pears reveal their colored layers with red on the outside and pearly white inside. All the fun is in deciding how to slice them and display them on the plate.

For 4 servings

- 4 pears
- 1 bottle red wine (750 ml)
- Generous 1 cup (250 g) white sugar
- Generous 3/4 cup (200 ml) blackberry cream
- 1 carton of raspberries in syrup (net weight once drained between 7 oz/200 g and 9 oz/250 g)
- 1/2 lemon

Peel the pears whole and keep the stem. In a pan, combine the red wine, generous 3/4 cup (200 g) sugar, and the blackberry cream. Add the pears and cook over medium heat for 30 minutes. Let cool in the pan (they can even stay there all day or overnight). Drain the raspberries and combine them with the juice of half a lemon and the rest of the sugar. Pass this puree through a fine strainer. Arrange the pears upright on a small plate and pour the coulis over them.

Carrot Bavarian creams with orange sauce

For 4 individual Bavarian creams

- 2 leaves gelatin
- 9 oz (250 g) carrots (+ 1 small one for decoration)
- 1 1/4 cups (300 ml) cream
- Scant 1/4 cup (50 g) tightly packed dark brown sugar

For the orange sauce

- 2 1/2 organic oranges
- Scant 2/3 cup (140 g) white sugar
- 4 eggs
- 7 tbsp (100 g) butter

Soften the gelatin in a bowl of cold water. Peel and slice the carrots. Cook them in boiling water for 20 minutes, then puree them. Place 2/3 cup (150 ml) of cream, the sugar, and the gelatin in a pan. Heat slowly, stirring all the time so that the sugar and gelatin melt; remove from the heat before it reaches a boil. Combine this cream with the carrot puree. Place in a mixing bowl and place in the refrigerator for 30 minutes. Beat the rest of the cream until stiff and blend into the chilled mixture. Place in ramekins and chill in the refrigerator for 4 to 5 hours.

To make the sauce, squeeze and strain the juice of 2 oranges. Beat 1/2 cup (120 g) sugar with 2 whole eggs and 2 yolks until the mixture turns pale. Pour the juice, egg, and sugar mixture, and the chopped butter into a pan. Cook over low heat, stirring all the time with a wooden spoon, until the cream thickens and coats the back of the spoon. Let cool. Using a zester or a vegetable peeler, peel some fine strips from the small carrot kept for the decoration. Peel the zest from the remaining orange half and squeeze out the juice. Place the strips of carrot in a pan together with generous 1 cup (250 ml) water, the orange juice, and the rest of the sugar. Boil until almost all of the liquid has evaporated. Combine these carrot strips with the orange zest which you had set aside. Turn the Bavarian creams out of the ramekins onto plates, pour the orange sauce over them, and decorate with orange zest and carrot strips.

Mango tarte tatin with rosemary

There must be thousands of tarte tatin recipes, each one of them claiming to be authentic. That it is exactly the kind of debate which does not interest us... In short, let's upset the purists and simply get rid of the apples! The cooked mangoes, or rather, caramelized mangoes, are the key. Especially if you combine them with the southern and somewhat Antillean flavor of rosemary. It is a herb which one could be using in a whole variety of sauces. Not always easy to find fresh in the stores it is, however, very easy to grow in a pot on the balcony. That is a little more difficult with mangoes...

For 6 servings

· 2 mangoes
· 12 tbsp (175 g) butter, softened
· Scant 1/4 cup (100 g) tightly packed raw sugar
· 1 1/2 cups (175 g) flour
· 2 sprigs fresh rosemary
· 1/3 cup + 1 1/2 tbsp (100 ml) cream

Peel and slice the mangoes. Melt 6 tablespoons (75 g) of butter in a small pan and add scant 1/4 cup (50 g) of the raw sugar. Pour this syrup into a pie dish. Spread the mango slices on top. Place in the oven (400 °F/200 °C). Combine the flour, the rest of the butter, and the rest of the raw sugar. Add a little water (about 1/4 cup + 2 teaspoons/70 ml) so that the dough has a homogenous pastry consistency. Roll out on a cutting board. Chop the rosemary. Remove the pie dish from the oven. Sprinkle the chopped rosemary over the mangoes. Place the rolled out dough on top, pressing the edges down with your fingers. Return to the oven and cook for an additional 30 minutes. Remove from the pie dish by turning the tart upside down onto a serving plate, decorate with cream, and serve while still warm.

Rhubarb and banana crumble with white chocolate nuggets

We love the way crumble just melts away letting your tongue plunge into the soft warmth of the compote: it's the same with all crumbles. In addition to the soft/crispy contrast emphasized by the cereal, this crumble also has the sweet-and-sour element: the nuggets of white chocolate are like islands of sugar in a sea of slightly acid rhubarb which slowly attacks your taste buds. A great combination.

For 6 servings
· 1 lb 2 oz (500 g) rhubarb (3 stalks)
· 3 bananas
· 1 3/4 cups (200 g) flour
· 7 tbsp (100 g) butter, softened
· Scant 1/4 cup (50 g) tightly packed dark brown sugar
· 1/3 cup (80 g) crispy breakfast cereal
· 3 1/2 oz (100 g) white chocolate
· 7/8 cup (100 g) confectioners' sugar
· Ground cinnamon

Peel the rhubarb and keep several long red strips for the decoration. Slice into pieces about the same size as the peeled bananas. Place the fruit in a pan and cook, covered, over gentle heat for 10 minutes, then remove the lid and cook for an additional 10 minutes until almost all of the juice has evaporated. In the meantime, prepare the crumble by mixing the flour, butter, dark brown sugar, and the cereal together with your fingertips. The dough should remain crumbly (this is helped by the inclusion of the cereal). Break the chocolate into small squares. Add the confectioners' sugar to the fruit. Pour into an ovenproof dish. Wait until cool before spreading the chocolate nuggets on top (if you do it straight away they will melt). Then spread the crumble on top and finally sprinkle with cinnamon. Place under the broiler for 10 minutes. Decorate with the red rhubarb strips and serve warm.

Ingredients or unexpected
liaisons

The mishaps

You never get to see behind the scenes, the mishaps, the failures, the dishes that stick, the sauces that curdle, and the fruit that gets burned… Precisely because we are not chefs and we do not have a reputation to preserve (but more especially, we admit, because it is funny), we show you our mess ups. It's up to you to complete them…

Concrete cannelloni
The filling for the first attempt (p. 88) was also comprised of pears but they were mixed with semolina and raisins. Durum wheat filled with durum wheat in effect! Not bad if you like the feeling of a brick in your stomach…

Harlequin by night
The recommended amount of agar-agar is 0.07 oz (2 g) (1 sachet) per 2 cups (500 ml) of liquid. You just have to read the instructions to know that… and which we didn't do, convinced that we could do it ourselves based on intuition. We therefore had to wait for 5 hours between each layer of color for them to set. That means more than 24 hours for a dish with five colors, including overnight, for a single glass! To ensure that nobody follows our example we have doubled the amount required.

Charcoal parsley

The sashimi tuna spaghetti (p. 152) is accompanied by cooked parsley. How do you cook parsley? By simply throwing it into the pan ... only to see it shrivel up and instantly turn as black as charcoal! It took several futile attempts before we realized that you need to blanch it first.

Steamed cuisine

"Eucalyptus-flavored Berber semolina." Sounds good, doesn't it? It meant cooking the semolina atop an infusion of eucalyptus leaves, as if inhaling the vapor, and serving it sweetened with yogurt. Except for the fact that, by the time we were finished, everything in the house smelt like a hospital...except the semolina!

Molotov apple

The idea of applying the cooking technique known as "deviled" to an apple (halfway between a tribal oven and a pressure cooker): keeping the fruit whole and covering it in a sort of quick-setting glue. The result of this badly managed condensation? The apple exploded, coating the interior of the oven with a grainy compote and a coagulated dough.

Chinese artichokes
with Camembert cheese

Here is how to make a change from potato chips and olives for snacking on with a glass of white wine! You will have everybody wide-eyed when you put the Chinese artichokes on the table, especially if you tell them they are Guatemalan caterpillars... Chinese artichokes are, in fact, the fleshy underground part of the stalk of a plant originally from Japan. They were introduced to Europe at the end of the 19th century and their very subtle taste becomes stronger when they are cooked in butter. For serving with an aperitif, however, we did not want to destroy their pretty Michelin-man shape.

For 4 servings
· 7 oz (200 g) Chinese artichokes
· Coarse-grain salt
· 9 oz (250 g) Camembert

Place the Chinese artichokes in a plastic bag with the coarse-grain salt. Shake the bag well to remove the thin, slightly gray skin by means of friction. Finish the peeling by hand if necessary (you don't usually need to because you can eat them as they are). Place the Chinese artichokes in boiling salted water and cook for 10 minutes. Drain and let cool. Bake the cheese in an ovenproof dish for 5 to 7 minutes in a hot oven (about 450 °F/230 °C) until melted slightly. Serve the Chinese artichokes with the cheese as a dip.

Jerusalem artichoke carpaccio with licorice

Jerusalem artichokes: discovered in Brazil in the 16th century they are to be found more and more readily at markets. So let's make the most of it! They can be cooked like potatoes: sautéed, boiled, or steamed, as French fries or as mashed potato. They also have an added bonus: they can also be eaten raw and that is when they really reveal their delicate nutty flavor. We decided to put them together with licorice to create a truly different taste duo...

For 4 servings

- 9 oz (250 g) small Jerusalem artichokes, very fresh (their skin should not be wrinkled)
- 4 tbsp nut oil
- 1 tbsp cider vinegar
- Salt and freshly ground black pepper
- 4 pinches licorice powder (you make this yourself by crushing a stick of licorice with a hammer, otherwise it is sometimes sold in pharmacies)
- Sticks of licorice for garnish (optional)

Peel the Jerusalem artichokes and then slice them very finely (you can use a vegetable peeler). Place them in a rosette shape on a plate without letting them overlap too much. Make a vinaigrette with the nut oil and cider vinegar. Sprinkle over the plate of Jerusalem artichokes. Season with salt and pepper and sprinkle with a pinch of licorice powder. Garnish with small sticks of licorice, if preferred.

Crispy salmon and coconut boats

The initial idea was to combine the soft raw salmon with something crunchy, or even better, crispy! We found the crunchy quickly enough: coconut, so seldom used fresh and which, like the salmon, has something fleshy about it. Some people even compare the taste of coconut milk to the taste of mother's milk. With this double dose of softness we needed quite a strong taste, something to wake up the tongue with a series of drum beats: shrimp potato chips, which practically explode in your mouth once they come into contact with saliva. In our first couple of attempts we crushed them hoping to obtain an explosive crumb mixture, but the crisps reveal their crispiness much better when you keep them whole.

For 20 boats

- 10 oz (300 g) salmon fillet, very fresh
- 10 cilantro leaves
- 2 tbsp lemon juice
- 2 tbsp olive oil
- 1 tsp ginger, ground or grated
- 1/4 of a fresh coconut
- Salt and freshly ground black pepper
- 1 or 2 packages shrimp potato chips

Chop the salmon into small cubes and finely chop the cilantro. Combine with the lemon juice, oil, and ginger. Remove the coconut flakes using a vegetable peeler, making sure you keep one piece intact for the garnish. Add the flakes to the mixture without crushing them. Cover the bowl and let them marinate in the refrigerator for half a day. When you are ready to serve them, stir the marinade, adjusting the seasoning with salt and pepper, and then place 1 tablespoon of the mixture on each shrimp potato chip. Garnish with a coconut flake. Serve immediately (after 30 minutes the chips start to become soft and lose their crispiness).

Pumpkin cream
with coconut and marzipan

Our lives would be all the poorer without the cucurbitaceae family. With their names, their shapes, and their gastronomic potential they are one of our favorites. This sweet-and-sour cream can be served as an appetizer or can be transformed into a dessert without a great deal of effort. After all, does the category matter? The original part is the marzipan which is used in little pieces more or less hidden in the sauce: you stumble across them as if they were sugared nuggets. As with anything different and with anything sweet, serve it in small quantities to create the effect without overdoing it.

For 4 small tasting servings
· 1 lb 2 oz (500 g) pumpkin
· 1 oz (25 g) marzipan
· 1/2 cup (125 ml) coconut milk
  (or coconut cream)
· 1 tbsp lemon juice
· Salt and freshly ground black pepper
· 1 pinch curry powder

Peel the pumpkin and chop into pieces. Steam for 15 minutes. In the meantime, prepare the marzipan nuggets by rolling into little balls. Set aside. Combine the pumpkin with the coconut milk (or coconut cream) and lemon juice. Adjust the seasoning with salt, pepper, and the curry powder. Reheat as required and serve in small bowls sprinkled with a few marzipan nuggets.

Foie gras with "chutney" and apple

The "chutney" is something of a neologism: a kind of red cabbage chutney in a raspberry vinegar and sugar mixture. Stored in a jar and covered with sunflower oil it will keep for several weeks in the refrigerator and can be served with cold meats and potato salads.

For 4 servings

· 1 small red cabbage
· 3 tbsp olive oil
· 5 tbsp dark brown sugar
· 5 tbsp raspberry vinegar
· Salt and freshly ground black pepper
· 4 leaves brik or phyllo pastry
· 4 handfuls of arugula
· 2 apples
· A little bit of butter
· 11 oz (320 g) raw foie gras (frozen is even better)

Chop the cabbage as finely as possible and place in a pan with 2 tablespoons of oil. Place on the stove over high heat for 5 minutes. Add the sugar and vinegar. Season with salt and a generous amount of pepper and cover with water. Cover and cook over gentle heat for 3 hours. Preheat the oven to 350 °F (180 °C). Fold the leaves of brik or phyllo pastry in four and cut them with scissors along the folds. Place them on a baking sheet in the oven to harden and brown at 300 °F (150 °C) for 5 minutes. Rinse and drain the arugula. Wash the apples and cut into thick slices (about 5/8 inch/1.5 cm), without peeling. Melt the butter in a skillet and cook the apple pieces for 5 minutes, turning them over so that they are well browned on both sides. Season with pepper. Do not wipe out the skillet, simply add the rest of the oil. Cook the foie gras, cut into 4 slices between 3/4 and 1 1/4 inches (2 and 3 cm) thick, for 2 minutes on each side. Season with salt and pepper. Assemble by alternating foie gras, apple, chutney, and arugula with a piece of brik or phyllo pastry between them. Serve immediately.

Licorice veal kebabs

Chewing on a piece of licorice brings back such happy childhood memories that we wanted to reinvent it in the adult version. Impregnating with medicinal oils by means of infusion served as our model: when crushed, the licorice flavors the olive oil in which it is marinated. Of course, this step can be simplified if you use licorice powder but this is not as easy to find as licorice sticks. Since the result is both delicious and different, start by preparing just small quantities for your guests. For a tasting, a single kebab per person is enough.

For 2 kebabs

· 2 sticks of licorice about
  8 inches (20 cm) long
· Olive oil
· 1 veal scallop
· Salt and freshly ground
  black pepper
· 1 shallot
· 1/3 cup (40 g) ground
  almonds

Using a knife, slice off a 2-inch (5-cm) piece from one end of each of the licorice sticks. Place the two smaller pieces in a plastic bag and crush them with a hammer. Set the two larger pieces aside. Pour 3 tablespoons of oil into a pan and add the crushed licorice. Heat for about 1 minute, switch off the heat as soon as it starts to bubble, and let infuse off the stove for 15 minutes (or longer). In the meantime, cut the veal scallop into very small cubes. Peel and chop the shallot as finely as possible. Strain the oil with the licorice (through a small tea strainer, for example). Combine the meat, the flavored oil, shallot, salt, and pepper and let marinate in the refrigerator for at least 2 hours. After 2 hours add the ground almonds and shape into kebabs around each stick. Carefully place each kebab in a skillet with a little oil (they are very fragile). Serve hot.

Tagliatelle with dulse seaweed and pine nuts

Ulva, himanthalia, wakame, kombu, porphyr, pioka, sea hair... Again, names which sound exotic without one even knowing what they are. And what are they? Edible seaweed of course. They are some of a dozen or so such seaweed, less well known in Europe and yet the basis of Japanese food. This recipe has been elaborated on and is based on dulse, a kind of iodine-rich seaweed with a very subtle taste. Its shape is similar to that of tagliatelle. The pine nuts (in keeping with the coastal theme...) add a sweet touch to this very flavorsome dish which can be prepared in a few minutes...

For 4 servings

- 5 oz (150 g) dulse seaweed (comes in a package in the refrigerated section of an organic grocery store, Asian grocery store, or a health food store)
- 12 oz (350 g) tagliatelle
- A little bit of butter
- 1 small bowl of pine nuts
- Generous 3/4 cup (200 ml) cream
- Salt and freshly ground black pepper

Place the seaweed in a strainer and hold under cold running water for a good 5 minutes. This is the best way to remove the grains of sand and to make it less salty. Cook the tagliatelle in a large amount of water for the time indicated on the packaging. Drain the seaweed, then brown in a skillet with butter for 5 minutes. Coarsely crush half of the pine nuts using either a mortar and pestle or a rolling pin (or even a glass bottle if necessary!). Heat the cream in a small pan (without letting it boil). Season very lightly with salt and more generously with pepper and then add both the crushed and the whole pine nuts. Combine the tagliatelle and the seaweed and pour in the cream with the pine nuts. Add a last sprinkling of black pepper before serving.

Roast sea bream with pomegranate juice

This recipe is a homage to a fantastic red mullet with pomegranate eaten at an exceptional little restaurant in Venice. It involves a bit of guesswork (it is difficult to get the recipe from an Italian chef when you do not speak a word of his language and he doesn't want to give it to you anyway) and a bit of adaptation. The red mullet has become a pink sea bream for obvious aesthetic reasons: we wanted to play around with the shades of color with the pomegranate pips.

For 4 servings
- 2 sea bream, each about 2 lb (1 kg)
- 4 tbsp olive oil
- 2 small garlic cloves
- 2 tbsp raspberry vinegar
- 4 sprigs of thyme
- 2 bay leaves
- Salt and freshly ground black pepper
- 1 pomegranate

If he doesn't do it anyway, ask your fish supplier to scale and clean the sea bream. Make a marinade with the oil, crushed garlic cloves, vinegar, thyme, and bay leaves. Pour over the fish and let rest in the refrigerator for 1 to 3 hours. Turn the sea bream over in the marinade from time to time so that the marinade soaks into both sides equally. Preheat the oven to 450 °F (230 °C) for 15 minutes. Reduce the temperature to 350 °F (180 °C), switch to the broiler position, and cook the fish, seasoned with salt and pepper, for 20 minutes. In the meantime, carefully peel the pomegranate and remove the pips (keeping a few aside for the garnish) from which to extract the juice. Strain them. As soon as they come out of the oven, lift the sea bream fillets onto a plate and pour the pomegranate juice over them. Garnish with the pips you had set aside. Serve with steamed potatoes.

Pumpkin verrines with ginger cake

The return of the pumpkin! And there is no need to wait until Halloween to enjoy it. Some people will tell you they don't like it, so don't tell them what is in these verrines: the pumpkin is camouflaged by the cream. And since it is also embellished with cinnamon and condensed milk there is every chance that they won't notice. As for the ginger cake, it provides a soft, flavorsome base with a little freshness and life. It's up to you to invent other variations based on this example...

For 6 small servings

· 1 lb 2 oz (500 g) pumpkin
  (or other squash)
· 10 tbsp condensed milk
· 2 tbsp ground cinnamon
· 4 slices ginger cake
· Cream

Peel and dice the pumpkin. Steam for 15 minutes and then mash with a fork. Add the condensed milk and the cinnamon. Let cool. Crumble the ginger cake and put into 6 glasses. When you are ready to serve, pour a little of the creamed pumpkin on top and then finish with a dollop of cream. Eat immediately with a teaspoon.

Chestnut fondants with white chocolate

We are used to pairing chestnuts with dark chocolate but white chocolate is often forgotten in recipes. This injustice is addressed with these foolproof and very quick fondants. You can also make them in small individual molds. If you do, reduce the cooking time a little (18 minutes). We have tested it with making 150 of them: it works and they taste great!

For 6 small fondants

· 4 tbsp (50 g) butter
· 5 oz (150 g) white chocolate
· 9 oz (250 g) chestnut puree
  (1 carton)
· 2 eggs
· 2 tbsp milk

Preheat the oven to 350 °F (180 °C). Melt the butter and 3 1/2 oz (100 g) of the white chocolate, broken into pieces, either in a pan over gentle heat or in a bowl in the microwave. Remove from the heat and add the chestnut puree, followed by the eggs. Divide this dough among 6 small nonstick ramekins (or little greased and floured molds), filling them to a maximum 1/2 full. Place in the oven and bake for 25 minutes (extend the cooking time if they do not come out of the molds after this time). Remove the fondants from the molds and let cool on a baking sheet. They should sink in the middle. Melt the rest of the white chocolate. Thin with the milk. Pour the sauce into the small dip in each fondant and serve. These fondants can be kept for several days without going stale. The sauce will go hard but still tastes good.

Caramel pineapple cream

For the dried pineapple slices
· 1 small pineapple

For 4 small pineapple creams
· 7 oz (200 g) pineapple, fresh or canned
· 3 eggs + 3 yolks
· Generous 3/4 cup (180 g) tightly packed dark brown sugar
· 10 tbsp (150 g) butter

For the caramel
· Scant 1/4 cup (50 g) white sugar
· 1 1/4 cups (300 ml) lowfat milk
· 2 egg yolks
· 2 tbsp (25 g) butter

Make the dried pineapple slices the day before: remove the rind from the small pineapple and take out the core. Cut into very fine slices and place them on a baking sheet. Cook in the oven at 201 °F (80 °C) for 3 to 4 hours. Turn the slices over halfway through the cooking time. Let cool for as long as possible (preferably overnight). Make the pineapple cream on the day. Put the pineapple pulp in a food processor and process. Beat the 3 whole eggs and the 3 yolks together with the brown sugar. Combine the pineapple with the beaten eggs in a pan. Add the butter, cut into pieces, and allow it to melt over gentle heat (the cream must not boil; if it does beat it again in the food processor), stirring continuously, for 5 minutes. Place in the bowls straight away and keep in the refrigerator. Place the sugar in a heavy-bottom pan, soften with a little water, and cook over gentle heat, stirring continuously, until the mixture turns a deep beige color. In the meantime, heat the milk in a pan. Once it is hot, pour it over the caramel, stirring all the time. Beat the egg yolks and place in another pan in a bain-marie, gradually pour in the hot caramel milk, stirring all the time. The cream will thicken after several minutes. Do not allow it to boil! Once it coats the back of the spoon add the butter, cut into small pieces, and continue stir again for 30 seconds. Pour the cooled caramel cream over the pineapple cream, decorating with the slices of dried pineapple.

Pink lentil cream with acorn syrup

Lentils have a naturally slightly sweet taste which we have simply amplified to make this very tasty cream dessert. We preferred to use acorn syrup instead of sugar because it is a bit like honey from the trees and we liked the idea of being able to eat trees! If you have guests, let them try and work out what they have in their bowls. There is a good chance that most of them will give up trying to guess…

For 4 servings
· 1 1/4 cups (250 g) pink lentils
· 1 1/2 cups (350 ml) milk
· Generous 1 cup (250 ml) acorn syrup
· 1 tbsp (15 g) butter

Place the lentils in a pan and cook over low heat as you would a rice pilaf, by adding 2 times their volume of water to 1 part lentil (in this case, 2 cups/500 ml of water). When all the water has been absorbed the lentils will have changed color (they will now be a transparent beige) and almost all of them will have burst. Add generous 1 cup/250 ml (a large glass) of water and then the milk. Once the liquid has almost disappeared, add the acorn syrup and the butter. Taste and add some more syrup if you want a sweeter taste, then mix everything together. Serve either hot or cold.

NB: for a lighter texture, replace the milk with cream (35% fat). Beat the cream until stiff and fold into the lentil puree in two stages (the first part normally and then fold the second part in with a fork). Pour into the bowls and keep cool before serving.

Pear and chocolate cannelloni

The combination of pears + chocolate is nothing new. What is newer is the idea of using pears to decorate cannelloni and serving chocolate fondue as an alternative to a tomato coulis! You can prepare the cannelloni in advance and serve them cold, coated with hot chocolate.

For 4 servings

· I tbsp (15 g) butter
· 2 pears, very ripe
· 1/8 cup (30 g) white sugar
· Generous 3/4 cup (200 ml) cream
· I tsp cornstarch
· 4 cannelloni
· 5 oz (150 g) semisweet chocolate

Preheat the oven to 350 °F (180 °C) and grease a baking sheet with I teaspoon (5 g) of butter. Peel the pears and cut into cubes (about 1/4 inch/0.5 cm square). Melt the rest of the butter in a skillet over medium heat. Add the diced pears and the sugar. Cook for 5 minutes and then add half (1/3 cup +1 1/2 tablespoons/100 ml) of the cream as well as the cornstarch. Reduce to a gentle heat, stirring all the time, until almost all of the cream has disappeared. You should have a firm, creamy, pear puree with pieces in it. Fill the cannelloni with this puree and place them on the buttered baking sheet. Cover with aluminum foil and bake in the oven for 15 minutes. Remove the aluminum foil and cook for an additional 20 minutes. In the meantime, prepare the chocolate sauce. Break the chocolate into small pieces and melt them in a bain-marie. Once they are melted, pour in the rest of the cream which had been kept aside. Stir. Once the cannelloni are cooked, put them on the plates and pour the chocolate sauce on top.

Experimental Techniques

What the pros say...

"Modernity in cooking? I prefer looking to the future because the present is already here. You need to **start with an artistic idea** (the coast, the rainforest...) and to use techniques which give it feeling. In this way cooking, too, has the chance to become an art different from the handicraft which it often is today (tradition, repetition). There are therefore grounds to hope that we will be crying from emotion while eating."

Hervé This

"In my restaurant, when a guest looks at his plate in silence, looks up at his companion, smiles, licks his lips, and eats with air of jubilation... I know that he has seen the same fragment of the universe that I saw. He enters the world I have created out of food and wine, out of light and matter, out of the synergies I have offered him, **he breathes new air**. And this inherent breathing in of the creation is the life of the work."

Michel Bras

"The challenge is not the culinary invention, but the **culinary art**. The aim of cooking is not to achieve admiring astonishment on the basis of a technological or scientific endeavor. Cooking adds value to that point where science doesn't go; it has its own objectives: the beauty, that is to say, the good, in eating. It is this beauty which opens up the field of experience, which stimulates the will to repeat a positive eating experience."

Pierre Gagnaire

"The dessert is the climax of the meal. I like to play with it as with a stage drama: it needs to be unusual, it needs to provide a contrast."

Pierre Hermé

"The word confound contains the word found. **Confound** as a definition for a group of components which, at that precise moment, do not bear any relation to one another? This would mean that some of the combinations which we consider to be good today would have confounded us yesterday. How marvelous it would be to create according to already defined norms but without them being the only parameter, and to seek novelty without this search being the only preoccupation!"

Ferran Adrià

Crunchy crackling grapefruit cocktail

We could have simply called it a grapefruit granita. But this one has a bit extra: you can hear it crackling! Do you remember the sachets of sugar from when you were little, and which used to explode on your tongue? They are much more difficult to find these days but the Crazy Dips brand makes candies using the same principle. You just have to crush them and sprinkle them into the granita. Since it is very cold you can keep it on your tongue for a while... just enough for the powder to have its taste and sound effect. Since it is invisible in the mixture, the surprise effect is guaranteed.

For 10 small glasses

· 1/3 cup + 1 1/2 tbsp (100 ml) sweet white wine
· 3 tbsp confectioners' sugar
· 1/2 pink grapefruit
· 2 Crazy Dips candies or anther brand of "popping candy"

The day before, pour the wine into a bowl. Add the confectioners' sugar and stir until it is completely dissolved. Scoop out the flesh from the grapefruit, without the pith, and break into pieces with your fingers into the bowl: there should not be any pieces left whole but it should not be just juice either. Put the bowl in the freezer overnight. On the day, break up the frozen liquid with a fork and half-fill the glasses with the mixture. Return to the freezer. Also in advance, prepare the crackling powder by crushing the candies to a coarse powder with some large pieces still in it (do not crush them too finely). When you are ready to serve, pour a little of the crackling powder into the glasses, fill them with the frozen mixture, and finish by sprinkling with more powder. Slip a teaspoon into each glass and serve.

Hot and cold cucumber au gratin

The idea came from the similar shapes of a cucumber and a roll of goat cheese. What if the one was to be a lid for the other? Their combination in salads is a classic. Some people serve it hot, some cold, this is our version. We just had to hide the nuts and an ice cube as a surprise...

For 4 servings

- 1 cucumber
- 4 sprigs of mint
- 2 tbsp crème fraîche or sour cream
- Salt and freshly ground black pepper
- 8 shelled nuts
- 4 small ice cubes (optional)
- 1/2 roll of goat cheese (1/3 cup/80 g)

Slice the unpeeled cucumber so that you have 4 rectangular pieces, each at least 1 1/2 inches (4 cm) long. Scoop out each piece using a teaspoon. Discard the seeds from the middle and put the rest of the flesh in a strainer. Continue to scoop them out until you almost reach the skin from the inside, taking care not to break through the bottom of the pieces because this has to be kept whole. Remove the mint leaves from the stalk, keeping the tips for the garnish. Place them in a food processor with the cucumber flesh. Mix together with the crème fraîche or sour cream. Season with salt and pepper. Fill the cucumber pieces with this mixture up to a maximum of 1/2 full. Push 2 nuts into each of them. Place in the refrigerator for at least 30 minutes. When you are ready to serve, submerge an ice cube in each piece of cucumber, making sure that they are very small (if not, leave them out). Cut 4 slices 1/2 inch (1 cm) thick from the roll of goat cheese. Place them on top of the cucumber pieces so that they stay slightly raised. Place the cucumber pieces on a baking sheet and place on the top shelf of the oven so that they are close to the broiler for 5 to 7 minutes, checking them frequently. Serve immediately, as soon as the cheese is browned and before the cucumber becomes too warm. Eat with a teaspoon.

Rum-marinated halibut
with an endive and candied fruit salad

This recipe was born on a New Year's Day due to the orange slices which had been marinated in the punch and a box of candied fruit which had been given to me. I have tried to put these alcoholic oranges into a number of dishes only to establish each time that there comes a point where their flavor is overtaken by the alcohol. The only option was then to create the recipe without the punch. As for the nuggets of candied fruit, they go marvelously with the bitterness of the endive.

For 2 servings

· 10 cilantro leaves
· 1/2 organic orange
· 2 tbsp rum
· 3 tbsp olive oil
· 1 tbsp lemon juice
· Salt and freshly ground black pepper
· 7 oz (200 g) halibut fillet
· 3 pieces of candied fruit
· 2 small endives (we used red but the white ones will also do)

Chop the cilantro. Slice the orange half. Remove the rind (easy to peel off a slice). Dice the flesh. Do the same with the fish. Place the orange—flesh and rind—in a bowl together with the rum. Cook in the microwave at maximum for 1 1/2 minutes. Add the oil, lemon juice, cilantro, salt, and pepper to the bowl and mix well. Add the fish and mix thoroughly. Cover with plastic wrap and let marinate in the refrigerator for at least 2 hours, stirring the marinade from time to time, if possible. After 2 hours, remove the orange rind and discard. Dice the candied fruit. Remove the best leaves from the endive and dice the rest. Add the chopped endive to the fish in the marinade. Divide the mixture among the endive leaves, sprinkle with the candied fruit, and serve.

Coca-Cola foam on bacon chips

You are busy asking yourself: is this good? OK, we know this isn't going to be for everyone. The reason we are including it here is because it is fun to simply experiment. The contrast between the lightness of the foam and the crispy bacon is striking. So is that between sweet and salty and is, in fact, a bit too much, hence the attempt to offset it by caramelizing the bacon. Let's say that this recipe is a work in progress. Perhaps you will be willing to continue?

For 4 chips

· 4 slices of bacon
· 1 tbsp honey
· 2 cups (500 ml) Coca-Cola, approx.
· 2 scoops vanilla ice cream

Fry the bacon in a skillet without any fat. Add the honey to caramelize it. Switch off the heat and let it cool. Pour the Coca-Cola into a whisky glass placed in a soup bowl. Put a very cold scoop of vanilla ice cream in the glass. A strange chemical process will take place: the production of a large amount of foam which you need to scoop up with a dessertspoon. We tried several (fascinating) different ways of furthering the process by adding ice cream and Coca-Cola to one another one step at a time. We produced a lot more than the 4 tablespoons of foam required. Place the foam on the caramelized bacon chips and eat straight away.

Variations: you can replace the vanilla ice cream with another flavor of ice cream so long as it is very cold. The same applies to the Coca-Cola which can also be replaced with another kind of fizzy pop. The end result is neater if you serve the foam on fruit chips rather than bacon chips. Try leaving apple slices to dry on the radiator for 24 hours on to see...

Scrambled eggs infused with smoked salmon and dill

Do you remember those science experiments when you investigated the porosity of egg shells by impregnating them with ink? Here the shells don't just allow liquids to pass through them but also flavors. We have used this natural porosity to flavor really fresh eggs. This means you can eat scrambled eggs with salmon and dill... without salmon and without dill! The same principle can be applied with truffles or perhaps with a strong-smelling cheese. The result is amazing: you can smell something in your mouth but you don't see it on your plate.

For 4 servings
· 1 bunch dill
· 4 slices of smoked salmon
· 12 really fresh eggs
· Generous 3/4 cup (200 ml) cream
· Salt and freshly ground black pepper
· A little bit of butter

Cover the base of an airtight box (such as Tupperware) with the bunch of dill. Cut the salmon into slices about 1 1/4 to 2 inches (4 to 5 cm) long. Wrap the eggs in these strips and place them on the bed of dill. Close the box and place in the refrigerator for 4 days or up to a week. Break the eggs and beat them with a fork as if for an omelet. Add the cream, season with salt, and stir again. Melt the butter in a skillet, pour in the eggs and cream, and cook for about 5 minutes, stirring all the time with a wooden spoon. Sprinkle with freshly ground black pepper and serve with an arugula or lettuce salad.

Mussels tartare with green apples

We think of eating mussels raw all too seldom. This is a shame because their flesh is smooth and the flavor even more subtle than oysters... For this recipe it is best to use Spanish mussels which are much larger and fleshier.

For 4 servings
· 16 Spanish mussels
· 1 Granny Smith apple
· 1 onion
· 1 lime
· Salt and freshly ground black pepper
· 8 tsp olive oil
· Coarse-grain salt

Wash the mussels under cold running water, carefully scooping them out with a knife. Fill a glass bowl with cold water and place them in there. Discard any which are not completely closed (this is why it is always a good idea to have a few more than you need). Open the mussels by cutting the muscle between the two halves of the shell (near the hinge). Remove the flesh and chop into pieces on a plate. Add the finely chopped apple and onion together with the juice of half the lime. Season with salt and pepper, pour in the oil, and stir. Refill the shells with this tartare. Slice the remaining half of the lime very finely, without removing the rind, and use them to garnish the shell halves resting on a bed of coarse-grain salt.

Cumin clouds

Being able to eat clouds, is that not a universal dream? A little like swimming in a pool of milk, crossing a river of honey, or visiting a gingerbread house... In this recipe, however, we are not asking you to catch a cumulonimbus, just to bring the softness of beaten egg whites into contact with a hot skillet, together with a little cumin as stardust and some cheese strands as celestial sheep. Light and full of flavor, the little balls which result go down particularly well with children who love eating the crispy softness without a knife and fork, simply crushing them with the tips of their fingers...

For 4 servings
· 2 whole eggs + 2 egg whites
· 7 oz (200 g) Gouda with cumin
· I small bowl (scant I cup/50 g) breadcrumbs
· Salt and freshly ground black pepper
· 3 or 4 sprigs of parsley
· 4 tsp ground cumin
· 5 tbsp olive oil

Separate the egg whites from the yolks. Beat the 4 egg whites until stiff. Grate the Gouda with cumin and place in a mixing bowl together with the beaten egg whites, I egg yolk, and 4 tablespoons of breadcrumbs. Season with salt and pepper, mix, and then shape into balls the size of a large walnut. Beat the remaining egg yolk in a soup bowl. On a plate next to the soup bowl, combine the rest of the breadcrumbs, the chopped parsley, and ground cumin. Roll the balls in the egg yolk and then in the breadcrumbs. Heat the oil in a skillet and brown the balls for 3 to 4 minutes. Place the balls on a piece of paper towel before serving as an aperitif together with a bowl of mayonnaise seasoned with I teaspoon ground cumin, or even as an appetizer with a green salad.

Porcini-flavored gnocchi without the porcini

The sources of inspiration when looking to experiment with new cooking techniques (at least, new for amateurs!) include the adjusting and adapting of techniques from other domains. Such as the perfume business. We had heard of hot and cold enfleurage, an ancient technique for capturing perfumes in a body of fat and which was known to the Ancient Egyptians. If it works with cosmetics why shouldn't it work with food aromas? This is the test we undertook with strongly flavored dried porcini and cream. Ultimately a very simple alchemy which results in a porcini-flavored cream... without any trace of porcini on the plate. You just have to be careful not to heat the cream too much because the mushrooms must not be allowed to cook.

For 4 servings
· 1 1/4 cups (300 ml) cream (not lowfat!)
· 1 tbsp (10 g) dried porcini
· 1 1/2 lb (700 g) gnocchi
· Salt and freshly ground black pepper
· 1 tbsp chives, chopped

Pour the cream into a small pan. Add the dried mushrooms and heat over gentle heat for 5 minutes, without letting it boil. Let infuse for 3 to 4 hours, then strain and discard the dried porcini (they no longer have any taste at all). Cook the gnocchi in boiling water for the time indicated on the packaging (2 to 3 minutes is usually enough). Drain the gnocchi and pour the cream over them. Season with salt and pepper and sprinkle with chives.

Teriyaki eggplant

Sweet and salty, teriyaki sauce is a seasoning for broiled meat in Japanese cuisine: hence one talks of "steak teriyaki." We have made the association with eggplant, cooked like a pilaf! Yes, pilaf as in rice, which allows it to absorb the flavors of the sauce. This recipe is the result of a number of adjustments…

For 4 servings

· 2 eggplants
· 3 tbsp olive oil
· 3 1/2 tbsp (50 ml) teriyaki sauce
· 12 oz (350 g) tagliatelle
· Salt and freshly ground black pepper

The result is very tasty, and a dish of pasta is its unusual accompaniment. It makes a pleasant change to bolognese and is not difficult to make.

Wash, wipe, and then slice the eggplants lengthwise into slices 3/4 inch (2 cm) thick. Heat 2 tablespoons of oil in a skillet and place the eggplant slices in it. Once they are well browned on one side, add the teriyaki sauce to the bottom of the skillet, turn the eggplants over, and cover with cold water. Stir carefully, reduce the heat, and cover. In the meantime, cook the tagliatelle for the time indicated on the packaging. The eggplants are cooked once all the water has been absorbed. They should be coated with a brown, caramel sauce. Drain the tagliatelle, add the rest of the oil, season with salt and pepper, stir again, and then place the eggplant slices on top. Deglaze the skillet with 2 or 3 tablespoons of water, stirring with a wooden spoon, and pour the sauce over the dish.

Variation: you can replace the 3 1/2 tablespoons (50 ml) of teriyaki sauce with the following combination: 1 tablespoon + 1 teaspoon (20 ml) light soy sauce, 2 teaspoons (10 ml) sake (or half one half pear liqueur), 2 teaspoons (10 ml) cider vinegar, 1 tablespoon dark brown sugar, and 1/2 teaspoon chopped fresh ginger.

Parsnip stalagmites
with catastrophe cheese

We really like this recipe because you never know what the outcome is going to be! Sometimes everything collapses and other times a veritable edible sculpture emerges from the oven. There is a trick, however, if you want to be a little more certain that you will impress your guests: cook the parsnips the day before and set them aside to dry at room temperature. Then they will stay firm until the final step (which you will do in the microwave in order to reheat the parsnips at the same time as melting the cheese). However, the visual spectacle is not the only attraction: it is a true taste experience because you will discover that the parsnips develop several flavors at once depending on the parts tasted, similar to turnip at the base, potato in the middle, and sweet potato at the tip... a miracle!

For 2 servings
· 4 small parsnips with inspiring shapes (not too elongated)
· Salt
· 2 3/4 oz (80 g) stale cheese

Scrub or peel the parsnips, making sure you keep them whole. You only need to cut off the base so that they have a flat surface. Place them in a large quantity of boiling, salted water and cook for 10 to 15 minutes depending on their size: pierce them with a knife to test if they are cooked. Drain them and stand them upright next to one another on a baking sheet. Cut the cheese into 4 cubes. Using the tip of a knife, make a conical hole in each of the cubes so that you can make them stick on the tips of the parsnips (not easy). Place the baking sheet in the oven at the broiler position for 5 minutes, or in the microwave for 2 minutes. Patch up the result by winding the strings of cheese around the parsnips. Do this quickly: it solidifies as soon as it starts to cool.

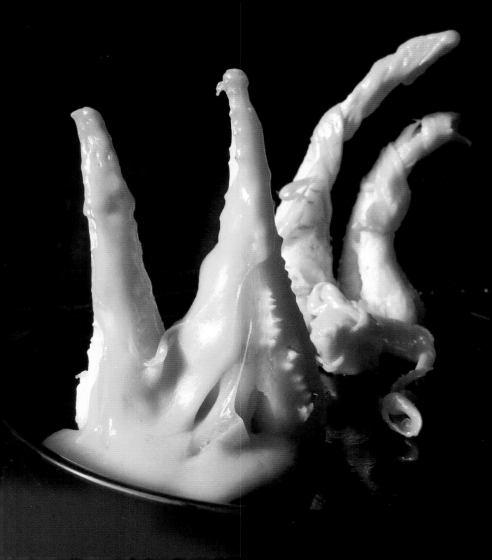

Wrapped cod with lemon verbena

Here is one of grandma's ingredients: verbena! Usually used as an infusion, there are two kinds: medicinal verbena, with serrated leaves, recommended for medicinal remedies, and lemon verbena, widely used for tisanes but with little effect. But what an aroma! Its Latin name is *Lippia citriodora*, where one can see the link to the lemon family. That is what gave us the idea to use it to flavor fish as you would lemon. The wrapping technique allows to give off its full aroma. You simply have to remove the leaves before serving when you remove the aluminum foil. Hmm ! That almost makes us want to cook with perfume. How about cod with the aromas of Guerlain or Dior?

For 1 serving
· 1 tbsp olive oil
· 1 cod fillet
· 1/2 shallot
· 1 1/4 oz (40 g) broccoli
  (a few little florets)
· 1 small handful of dried
  lemon verbena leaves
· 1 tsp lemon juice
· Salt and freshly ground
  black pepper

Preheat the oven to 400 °F (200 °C). Cut off a large piece of aluminum foil. Pour the oil in the middle and place the fish fillet on it. Peel and chop the half shallot. Sprinkle over the fish. Spread the broccoli and the lemon verbena leaves over the fish. Sprinkle with lemon juice. Season with salt and pepper. Wrap up the foil so that it is sealed. Bake in the oven for 20 minutes. Serve immediately.

NB: we have also tried it with a sprig of dried lavender but the result was incredibly strong. You have to be a real Provence fan to enjoy that…

Spicy smoked tuna steak

We have had a traditional Chinese recipe for smoked chicken in our heads for a long time. However, the unforgettable experience of a mysterious "tuna smoked with black herbs" at Jean Chauvel's restaurant Les Magnolias (our favorite) managed to get us going. After several experiments, some of which were almost inedible, especially if anise was involved for even just for a few minutes, we achieved a result which was original enough to be included here. The tuna takes on the flavor of the spices in very little time and also absorbs the smoke... cooking at the same time. We are a long way off Jean Chauvel's skills, but are still satisfied that we tried!

For 1 serving
· 1 star anise (+ 1 for the garnish)
· 5 peppercorns
· 1 tbsp white sugar
· 1 tuna steak, very fresh, without the skin

Crush the star anise and peppercorns. Line the bottom of a pan with 4 layers of aluminum foil and add the crushed spices and sugar. Place a marguerite (a metal basket used for steaming) on top. Put a piece of baking parchment in the middle (to prevent the tuna from sticking to the holes in the marguerite). Place the tuna steak on the paper. Switch on the heat. The sugar will soon melt and caramelize. As soon as smoke appears, cover with an airtight lid and watch the time: for the tuna steak to be cooked on one side and still somewhat raw on the other work on 5 minutes; for a well-cooked tuna steak which is still tender, work on 10 minutes. Thereafter the tuna will become very dry.

Agar-agar harlequin

Agar-agar is a marvelous gelling agent based entirely on seaweed. Not only is it more reliable than those usually available in the stores (and which are also based on pork carcasses!), its very rapid setting time means you can play around with layers and colors... It is sold as a powder in organic food stores.

For 2 glasses

· 1/3 cup + 1 1/2 tbsp (100 ml) strawberry juice
· 1/3 cup + 1 1/2 tbsp (100 ml) coconut milk
· 1/3 cup + 1 1/2 tbsp (100 ml) lemon juice
· 1/3 cup + 1 1/2 tbsp (100 ml) cherry juice
· 1/3 cup + 1 1/2 tbsp (100 ml) raspberry juice
· 0.021 oz (6 g) (3 × 2 g sachets) agar-agar powder

In a pan, heat the strawberry juice with half a sachet of agar-agar (about 0.035 oz/1 g). Stir continuously, then remove from the heat before it boils and pour into the glasses. While the liquid cools and starts to set (15 to 30 minutes), do the same again with the next juice. Once the glasses are full place them in the refrigerator for as long as possible (at least 2 hours, preferably overnight), before eating with a teaspoon.

Variation: you can, of course, allow your imagination to have free reign and make this Harlequin with the juice of any fruit. You can also include pieces of fruit to set in the agar and which will then be transparent.

Banana and mango makis

The trick to this optical illusion: you put the unpeeled banana pieces in the oven for 15 minutes so that their skins blacken and turn exactly the same color as nori seaweed which is what is used for real makis. The skin also means they are cooked in a kind of vacuum which makes the flesh very tender.

For 4 servings
- 4 bananas
- 1 mango
- 4 tbsp dark brown sugar
- A little bit of butter

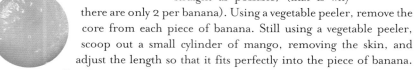

Preheat the oven to 450 °F (230 °C). Cut two equal-size pieces (about 1 1/2 inches/4 cm) from each banana, as straight as possible, (that is why there are only 2 per banana). Using a vegetable peeler, remove the core from each piece of banana. Still using a vegetable peeler, scoop out a small cylinder of mango, removing the skin, and adjust the length so that it fits perfectly into the piece of banana.

Put the sugar on a small plate and roll the cylinders of mango in it before sliding them into the holes at the center of the banana pieces. Butter a baking sheet and place the banana pieces upright on it. Reduce the oven temperature to 350 °F (180 °C) and bake the makis for 15 minutes. Eat hot or cold with a teaspoon.

Variation: for an adults only version soak the mango cylinders in a glass of rum before rolling them in the sugar.

Chocolate mousses served according to chocolateness

OK, "chocolateness" is an invented word but we needed it in order to be able to name this experience. The difference between eating and tasting is often a question of ritual. We are suggesting that you taste three chocolate mousses in the order corresponding to their cocoa content. Both decadent and delicious.

For 4 servings
· 4 eggs, very fresh
· 1/3 cup (40 g) confectioners' sugar
· 2/3 cup (150 ml) cream (not lowfat, i.e. with 35 % fat)
· 2 1/4 oz (70 g) bittersweet chocolate with 51% cocoa
· 2 1/4 oz 70 g) bittersweet chocolate with 70% cocoa
· 2 1/4 oz (70 g) bittersweet chocolate with 85% cocoa
· 3 tbsp strong coffee

Separate the egg whites from the yolks. Beat the egg whites until stiff. Sprinkle with confectioners' sugar and beat for about an additional 1 minute. The mixture should be both firm and shiny. Beat the cream until as stiff as possible. Carefully combine the cream with the beaten egg whites. Beat the 4 egg yolks in a mixing bowl and then divide equally among 3 large bowls (it is a good idea to number them by sticking a a small sticker on each of them). Melt the chocolate with 51% cocoa in a bain-marie, then combine it with the egg yolk and 1 tablespoon of coffee in the first bowl. Using a fork, carefully fold in one-third of the egg white and cream mixture, taking care that the mousse does not collapse. Cover with plastic wrap and place in the refrigerator. Do the same with the 70% chocolate and then with the 85% chocolate Serve in 3 large bowls or 3 little glasses, indicating the tasting order (from the least cocoa up to the most cocoa).

Malva gelatin dessert
with apple and condensed milk

Having once visited a herbalist we have learned that it is possible to obtain all manner of dried edible flowers in a number of towns. They are sold for their therapeutic properties but there is nothing to stop you using them for culinary experiments. The point of departure for this one is simply the aesthetic pleasure of working with a lovely violet blue infusion. The result is more unusual than delicious but the process makes it worth trying.

For 6 servings

· 3 leaves gelatin
· 2 small handfuls of dried malva (mallow)
· 3 tbsp confectioners' sugar
· 1 tbsp honey
· 1 acidic apple
· Juice of 1/2 lemon
· 6 tbsp condensed milk

The day before, soften the gelatin in a small bowl of cold water. Heat generous 1 cup (250 ml) of water and remove from the stove as soon as it starts to bubble. Pour the water on the malva leaves (the color will change from blue to mauve in a few seconds). Let infuse for 10 minutes. Optional: strain the flowers and set aside on a piece of paper towel, sprinkle with confectioners' sugar, and roll them in it gently so that they absorb it, then put them on a marguerite (metal basket used for steaming) and place the marguerite on a working radiator. Dissolve the gelatin and the honey in the infusion. Let set overnight.

On the day, cut up the apple into thin sticks, without peeling, and sprinkle with the lemon juice. Fill 6 glasses one-third full with the malva gelatin. Stick several thin apple sticks in each glass. Pour 1 tablespoon of condensed milk into each glass. Top off with gelatin. Finish with several of the malva flowers dried on the radiator. Serve immediately.

Tomato skin tarts
with meadowsweet cream

These little tarts are a pastoral combination of tomato and meadowsweet. The tomato, only the skins of which are used, is transformed into delicate, crispy, honeyed petals. If you cannot find dried meadowsweet which is usually available in organic food stores or herbalists, you can always replace it with a vanilla bean.

For 4 servings
· 4 tomatoes
· 3 tbsp runny honey
· I ready-made puff pastry
· 2 cups (500 ml) milk
· 1/4 cup (50 g) sugar
· 2 tbsp dried meadowsweet
· 4 egg yolks

Place the tomatoes in boiling water for 3 minutes, then refresh them under the tap. Make a cross-shaped incision with a knife and remove the skin in 4 pieces. Cover them in honey and place on a baking sheet lined with baking parchment. Place in the oven at 201 °F (80 °C) for 3 hours. Once the tomato petals are ready, remove them from the oven and increase the temperature to 450 °F (230 °C). Roll out the puff pastry to make it a little thinner. Cut out 4 rectangles from the pastry and place them on the baking sheet (change the baking parchment). Prick them with a fork. Reduce the oven temperature to 350 °F (180 °C) and cook for 15 to 20 minutes, turning them over halfway through cooking. If the pastry rises simply push it down again with the back of a fork. Bring the milk to a boil with the sugar and the meadowsweet; let infuse off the stove for 30 minutes, then strain. Beat the egg yolks and combine with the sugared milk. Strain. Allow to thicken in a bain-marie for about 5 minutes. Let cool. Assemble the tarts by spreading them with a layer of cream first of all, then place several tomato skins on each.

Tagada Medusas transformed with vodka

Here we move away from cooking toward the chemistry of the sorcerer's apprentice. The recipe is simplicity itself: you simply let a candy absorb alcohol until it completely changes texture. The rather brittle Fraise Tagadas are transformed into a malleable sponge while jelly candies triple in size in an also magical fashion. Are they good for your health? Definitely not. Do they taste good? They taste very unusual. Either way, we have tested them on a number of people and the strangeness of this recipe is always a success. That is also why we have give the amounts for 10 people, for serving at a party. We have even had a bar asking us for our secret!

For 10 servings
· 10 Fraises Tagadas
  (or other brittle candies)
· 10 small glasses vodka
  (very small…)

Several days in advance, place a Fraise Tagada at the bottom of a very small glass. Fill 3/4 full with vodka. Cover with plastic wrap and set aside… Serve either on a spoon or remove the inflated candy and present it on a plate. Caution: the candy changes a lot over a period of days. After a few days it becomes a malleable sponge. After 1 week it tends to dissolve in the alcohol and form a mousse-like jelly (see our photo). If you wait longer or if there is too much vodka, the candy dissolves completely and you have a deep pink liquid with a strong aroma which can be served as a cocktail. Do a number of tests to decide which consistency you prefer.

It's all in the decoration

Other ideas to develop

We have some three thousand and have chosen only about sixty for this book. Here are a few more to be read for fun like a menu and, more especially, for you to try out and even develop further yourself...

Tea-flavored tuiles in which you can see little transparent leaves.

A sweet compote of black beans, served warm with ice cream.

A cake baked in a can in order to be able to cut completely round slices.

Sprigs of fresh rosemary dipped in cheese fondue, for sucking on. Or chocolate?

Roast pork stuffed with whole candies.

Little foie gras pancakes with chestnut puree.

A pool of sugared fruit in beer and spices.

Poached fruit with a licorice coulis.

A basil sabayon for serving with a fresh strawberry salad.

Lotus flower chips, really pretty.

Melted ice cream as a sweet sauce.

Vegetables sautéed in a wok and coated with mixed fruit (mango?).

A smooth nettle sauce, just for the concept…

A savory floating island, foie gras in a lentil soup for example.

A transparent candy made from tomato pulp, completely clear so that the pips are visible.

Cucumber with salmon caviar and a green apple sauce

These are very refreshing little snacks which are slightly acidic due to the green apple sauce. They are even better if you keep them in the refrigerator for about 20 minutes before serving.

For 4 servings
· 1 cucumber
· 1 small jar of salmon caviar
· 2 Granny Smith apples
· 1 lime
· lemon juice

Wash the cucumber but do not peel. Cut into 4
pieces each 21/4 inches (6 cm) long. Cut these in two lengthwise, then scoop out the seeds, leaving the flesh, so that they form small containers. Fill with the salmon caviar lightly sprinkled with lemon juice. Peel the apples and mix with the juice of the lime. Assemble on the plates by placing the cucumbers on top of the apple sauce.

Black mushroom orchids with crispy bacon stamen

Dried black mushrooms, that is, strongly flavored mushrooms, are no longer the preserve of Asian delicatessens only: you can find them in any grocery store these days. Very easy to use, they make wonderful flower shapes once they rehydrate. With their slightly sticky texture they make a delicious contrast to the crispiness of the bacon.

For 4 servings
· 4 large black Chinese mushrooms
· 4 slices of bacon
· 2 little bits of butter
· Freshly ground black pepper
· 4 tbsp thick crème fraîche or sour cream
· 16 pink peppercorns

Soak the mushrooms in a bowl of warm water. They will triple in volume in 5 minutes. Drain and wipe with kitchen towel. Cut the bacon into fine strips about 1 1/2 inches (4 cm) long and 1/2 inch (1 cm) wide. Brown the bacon strips in a skillet with a little bit of butter. Season with pepper but not salt (the bacon is enough). Set aside on a plate. Do not wipe out the skillet, add the rest of the butter, reduce the heat, and cook the mushrooms whole for 5 minutes. Set them aside again. Still using the same skillet, heat the crème fraîche or sour cream for 1 minute. Stir with a wooden spoon in order to deglaze the skillet. Assemble the dish: place one mushroom in the center of each individual plate with 1 tablespoon of crème fraîche or sour cream. Stick the bacon strips in the crème fraîche or sour cream as if they were the stamen of a flower. Garnish with pink peppercorns.

Landscape on brioche parchment with bright sunlight

This recipe went around in our heads for several weeks before it was finished. The idea started with a brioche meant for a child, "cupped" in your hand so that it doesn't drop crumbs. The result had a new and interesting consistency. Then we also remembered the taste of a brioche we had eaten in Arles, semisweet and filled with warm goat cheese. And then the taste of Breton buckwheat galettes which have a raw egg yolk as the sauce. In the end, we wanted to evoke the age-old painters' technique of using egg white to hold their canvasses in place as well as children's drawings in which the sun is always completely round, perched at the top of the page. The result is the perfect recipe for a cooking session with children...

For 1 serving

· 1 slice ready-made brioche, precut
· 1 egg
· Herb and spices (dill is very practical)
· 1 tbsp grated cheese

Flatten the slice of brioche with a rolling pin, pressing it down hard. Turn it over (the picture is often prettiest on the other side). Separate the egg white from the yolk, taking care not to break the yolk. Brush a little of the egg white over the upper surface, either with a brush or with the tip of your finger: this makes everything stick. Create a landscape with the herbs and spices, pressing the pieces into the brioche. Put the grated cheese into a nonstick skillet. Add 1 or 2 tablespoons of egg white. Place the brioche on top so that it absorbs some of the mixture and heat slightly. Allow to cook for 1 minute, then remove it with a spatula. Slide the slice into a serving plate. Use the back of a spoon to make a dip where you want to put the sun. Slide the egg yolk into the dip as the sun. Serve immediately.

Alfalfa garden on a plate

Alfalfa is simply Lucerne, as it is sometimes called in organic food stores. It can be replaced by all sorts of germinating seeds: radish, lentils, fenugreek, cabbage, wheat, sunflowers, carrot, fennel, groundnuts... Mustard seeds, cress, and arugula have the inconvenience of needing to be grown on warm, moist cotton batting: not so practical on a plate. A fascinating recipe to have the children make: you can watch it growing everyday, its amazing. And really healthy, lots of proteins and trace elements!

For 4 servings

- 4 tbsp Lucerne seeds/alfalfa (or other germinating seeds)
- 5 oz (150 g) feta cheese
- Olive oil
- 1/4 cup (30 g) nuts or chopped nuts
- 1 avocado, not too ripe
- Lemon juice
- Salt and freshly ground black pepper

One week in advance, sprinkle the seeds on a large plate which is to be the serving plate (it is better not to have to move the seeds once they have germinated if you want to create the impression that they have grown there, but it is possible). Water them morning and evening without letting them dry out, but do not over water them either. Once they are well sprouted, cut a pathway through them with a knife. Crumble the feta, add a drop of oil, and then the nuts, then pave the pathway with this mixture. Peel the avocado, cut it in two, remove the pit, and cut one of the halves with a knife to form a small reservoir, the cavity of which is the whole left by the pit. Drizzle with lemon juice. Make a lemon vinaigrette and pour this into the reservoir. Cut the rest of the avocado into thin strips and find a place for them in the garden. Serve and eat from the serving dish, watering the sprouts with the vinaigrette from the reservoir.

Pear terrine with blue cheese and pink peppercorns

There is nothing special about the combination but the presentation is attractive. Many painters in the past have used the pear as a source of inspiration. It makes you want to give it the place of honor in the center of the plate. When mashed its flesh gives up a lot of juice. The ginger cake is there to absorb it and to give the filling a bit of body.

For 2 servings
- 2 pears
- 3 slices of ginger cake
- 5 pink peppercorns
- 2 black peppercorns
- 1 1/4 oz (40 g) blue cheese
- 2 nuts, chopped
- 1 tbsp raisins

Slice off the base of each pear so that they can stand up straight. Cut of the tops of the pairs, about a quarter of the way down. Scoop out the larger piece with a teaspoon. Cut two disks from the ginger cake in the right shape to fit the base of the scooped out pears. Slide these disks into the pears. Crush the pink and black peppercorns with a mortar and pestle. Combine with the blue cheese and the pear flesh, coarsely mashed with a fork. Add the nuts, raisins, and the last slice of ginger cake, crumbled. Fill the pears with this mixture. Place in the refrigerator for 30 minutes before serving.

Pink spaghetti with Romanesco cabbage

We said it at the start of the chapter: it's all in the decoration! This pasta salad is not going to amaze fans of subtle tastes: it is simply pretty. But cooking also serves to show hasty eaters that the world is beautiful if you take a look at what is on your plate. The uniform pattern of the Romanesco cabbage (an infinite symmetry) fascinates us: we wanted to do it justice without damaging the florets. And then, the coloring properties of beet are extraordinary to work with, especially when used to transform something as banal as pasta. It is the perfect salad for a casual party with just a few people: you can even put it in little disposable plastic cups, it is quick to make and costs next to nothing.

For 6 servings

· 5 oz (150 g) spaghetti
· Salt and freshly ground black pepper
· Olive oil, strongly flavored
· 1 cooked beet
· 6 tbsp fromage blanc
· Lemon juice
· Chives
· 6 small florets of Romanesco cabbage

Cook the spaghetti in boiling salted water until al dente and drain. Pour a generous amount of oil over them straight away so that they do not stick together and mix in carefully, without breaking them. Squeeze the beet in a cloth over the dish of spaghetti: dark pink juice will run out very easily and will color the pasta permanently (even if you rinse them they will stay pink). Mix in and let cool. Prepare the sauce by seasoning the fromage blanc with the lemon juice, salt, and pepper, and then blend in the chopped chives. The sauce needs to be fairly light. Place 1 tablespoon of sauce at the bottom of each glass, then a small pile of spaghetti so as to form a nest. Stick a small floret of Romanesco cabbage in the middle of each nest.

Giant mushroom water lilies on an avocado lake

In the magnificent film *Les Glaneurs et la glaneuse*, **Agnès Varda is fascinated by the bizarre beauty of malformed potatoes, especially the double ones shaped like hearts. If you take a stroll through the pick-your-own farms you will also find amusing natural anomalies in each furrow which are nowhere to be found on the grocery store shelves. Sometimes these examples of gigantism become a food fad, such as certain strangely over-dimensional mushrooms. The first idea would have been to stuff them but then you would lose the unusual sight of their fins which make them so attractive. These ones are therefore turned upside down and transformed into flowers on a minted green lake...**

For 2 servings

· 1 vegetable bouillon cube
· 10 mint leaves (+ several for garnish)
· 2 avocados, very ripe
· 2 tbsp crème fraîche or sour cream
· 2 pinches ground cumin
· Lemon juice
· Salt and freshly ground black pepper
· 2 mushrooms, as large as possible

In advance, dissolve the bouillon cube in generous 1 cup (250 ml) hot water and let cool. Chop the mint leaves. Combine the avocado flesh with the crème fraîche or sour cream, chopped mint, cumin, and just enough bouillon to obtain the desired smooth sauce consistency. Season with lemon juice, salt, and pepper. Peel the mushrooms, remove the stalk (will not be used). Sprinkle with a little lemon juice. Pour the avocado sauce into two soup bowls and place the mushrooms upside down on top.

Carambola starfish in orange sauce

Of course they are not real starfish, which are inedible as far as we know, but rather carambola ones, that exotic fruit used to garnish punch and fruit salads. However, it doesn't only have to be used for decoration. Once cooked it makes a fleshy and slightly acidic accompaniment for fish and shellfish. The thick orange sauce is a delicacy in itself. It is a little demanding because you have to make it at the last minute without leaving the stove but it doesn't take long. To be reused for other fish dishes.

For 2 servings

- 1/2 orange
- 1 carambola
- 1 egg yolk
- 4 1/2 tbsp (60 g) butter
- 2 tbsp crème fraîche or sour cream
- Salt and freshly ground black pepper
- Oil
- 6 scallops

Squeeze the juice from the orange half and remove the zest. Place in boiling water and blanch for 10 minutes. In the meantime, wash and slice the carambola. Place the egg yolk in a bain-marie (a pan inside another pan of hot water). Beat with 1 tablespoon of water. Add the butter and beat while it melts. Once the sauce has thickened slightly, add the crème fraîche or sour cream, the drained zest, and the orange. Adjust the seasoning with salt and pepper and let cook over gentle heat. In the meantime, brown the carambola slices on both sides in a skillet with a little oil. Add the scallops which only need to be cooked briefly. Switch off the heat. Beat the sauce once more with a fork (it will be lighter if you use an electric whisk), then pour it onto the plates. Place the carambola and the scallops on top. Serve immediately.

Mini country custards
with broccoli and Gorgonzola

**From the outside you would say like a sandcastle on the beach, a wobbly noth-
ing, fragile and solid at the same time. On the inside, it is a miniature for-
est, a tree surrounded by softness. We like surprise dishes: this is reminiscent
of the beans in the galette, birthday presents wrapped several times, chocolate
eggs with a little toy inside. Cooking as a present...**

For 4 servings

· 14 oz (400 g) broccoli
· 2 3/4 oz (80 g) Gorgonzola
· 2 tbsp crème fraîche or sour cream
· 2 eggs
· Salt and freshly ground black pepper

Split the broccoli into small florets and steam them for 10
minutes. Preheat the oven to 400°F (200°C).
Combine the Gorgonzola, crème fraîche or sour cream,
and the eggs. Keep 4 nice broccoli florets aside and add
the rest to the mixture. Season with salt and pepper. Pour
the mixture into small nonstick ramekins, filling them half
full. Place a broccoli floret in each of them, upside down.
Cover with the rest of the mixture. Cover the ramekins with aluminum foil and cook in a bain-marie in the oven for 25 minutes. Serve warm, as
an appetizer or as a side dish.

Sashimi tuna spaghetti with fried parsley

Fried parsley is used in the big restaurants to garnish fish dishes: sole meunière or turbot in beurre blanc. Here we have combined it with finely chopped raw fish. Ginette Mathiot meets Japanese cuisine…

For 4 servings
· 1 lb 2 oz (500 g) raw tuna, very fresh
· 1 bunch of curly parsley
· 4 tbsp olive oil
· Salt and freshly ground black pepper

Remove the skin and bones from the tuna (with a pair of tweezers), then place in the freezer for 1 hour; it will then be much easier to slice. Using a very sharp knife, slice the tuna into very thin long strips. Plunge the parsley into boiling water for 15 seconds. Drain and put into a bowl of ice cubes straight away; it will keep its green color this way. Drain, then dry carefully. Chop coarsely and then fry in hot oil for a few seconds. Season generously with salt and pepper. Place the tuna around the fried parsley in the shape of a nest.

NB: this dish can be served in the Japanese style with soy sauce and wasabi, or in the French style with slices of toasted bread and butter.

Strawberries filled with kiwi cream

You may prefer Gariguette strawberries or the little Mara des Bois with their strong flavor… But for this recipe you simply have to use the large Spanish strawberries. Grown under glass they are available practically the whole year round. So much the better because this means you can eat strawberries in almost any season!

For 4 servings
- 6 kiwi fruit
- Generous 1/4 cup (30 g) confectioners' sugar
- 2/3 cup (150 ml) cream (35% fat content)
- 12 large strawberries

Peel the kiwi fruit. Slice 3 of them into 4 slices 1/4 inch (0.5 cm) thick. You will need 12 slices which will be the bases for the strawberries. Cut the remaining kiwi fruit into small pieces and put them in a food processor. Strain them using a fine strainer. Sweeten the pulp once the seeds have been removed (you can do as we did and keep 1/2 teaspoon for the decoration). Beat the cream until stiff (this is much easier if both the cream and the bowl are very cold), then fold into the sweetened kiwi fruit puree. Remove the stalk from each strawberry and slice off the ends so that they sit straight. Scoop them out using the tip of a knife and then a teaspoon (or a grapefruit spoon). Place each strawberry on a slice of kiwi fruit and decorate with the kiwi cream. Keep in the refrigerator until ready to serve.

Banana, avocado, and mango millefeuille with a lemon and dill sauce

This is a dish which can be served either as an appetizer or at the end of the meal. It is based on a soft, gentle harmony. The lemon cream with dill invigorates the dish with its strongly acidic flavor. A refreshing bonus. Use mini tartlet molds which to give them the dainty shape.

For 4 servings

- 1 lemon
- 2 eggs
- 1/4 cup (50 g) white sugar
- Scant 4 tbsp (50 g) butter
- Few sprigs of dill
- 1 avocado
- 1 mango
- 2 bananas

To make the lemon and dill cream, squeeze the lemon and strain the juice. Beat the 1 whole egg and 1 yolk with the sugar until the mixture turns pale. Pour into a pan with the strained lemon juice and the butter, cut into small pieces. Melt over gentle heat, stirring all the time. The mixture will thicken after several minutes. Switch off the heat and let the cream cool before adding the finely chopped dill. Cut the avocado, mango, and bananas into uniform shapes and sizes and place them on top of one another. You can use a mold for this. Place a little of the flavored cream on each millefeuille and serve immediately. If you are not yet ready to serve, sprinkle a little lemon juice over each piece of fruit so that they do not turn brown.

Individual strawberry volcanoes

This one is thanks to Felix, 4 1/2 years old. "Mommy, how can you make a volcano that you can eat?" An interesting challenge: we took a chocolate chestnut fondant recipe which has the distinct advantage that you can shape it after cooking thanks to the elasticity of the chestnut puree. The result might not be perfect but what mountain is, especially in the middle of a volcanic eruption?

For 6 servings

- 5 oz (150 g) semisweet chocolate
- Scant 4 tbsp (50 g) butter
- 9 oz (250 g) chestnut puree (1 carton)
- 1 egg
- 1 carton of strawberries
- Cocoa powder
- Birthday candles

Preheat the oven to 350°F (180°C). Melt the chocolate and the butter. Add the chestnut puree, then the whole egg. Mix well. Pour the mixture into nonstick ramekins and bake in the oven for 25 minutes. Remove from the molds and let cool. Turn each cake upside down, stick your finger into the middle to make a crater, and shape into a mountain. Sprinkle with cocoa powder to hide the faults. Put the strawberries through the food processor. Put a little strawberry coulis in the middle of each crater, letting it run down like lava. Place a birthday candle in the summit (shorten them if necessary) and serve immediately.

The origin of this book

Anna Pavlowitch and Raphaële Vidaling first met at a brainstorming organized by Raphaële and Frédéric Ploton for the writing of their book *30 x 30: 900 Projects for Thirty Year Olds* (Tana éditions, 2003). It was about finding obscure ideas for doing big things with your life: 30 ideas for novels to write, 30 ideas for restaurants to open, 30 ideas to start a business, etc. The two women realized that they were on the same creative wavelength.

Anna is originally a philology teacher and Raphaële a language teacher. Both of them ended up in publishing, Anna as literary editor, Raphaële as novelist, author of illustrated books and, more recently, culinary photography for this series which she has directed: "My Grain of Salt."

apavlowitch@free.fr

raphaele.vidaling@laposte.net

Raphaële had the idea of a thoroughly inventive cookbook in her head for a long time, despite her relative culinary imperfection: a repertoire of attractive, experimental ideas. She had wanted to put together a circle of friends as "explorers of culinary inventions," amateurs who would get together once a month to taste new homemade dishes. She told Anna about this (it was one of the 900 projects). A few days later, Anna had already put together a few recipes intended for this dinner among friends!

She was therefore the one Raphaële turned to without hesitation to help complete this book, which they ended up sharing equally, each in their own kitchen, getting together to taste and photograph the dishes.

Our thanks are due to the first guinea pigs: Benoît, Rémi, Félix, and Noé …